BASEBALL WISDOM

What the Game Teaches Us

Library of Congress Cataloging-in-Publication Data:
Benson, John

Baseball Wisdom
1. Baseball — United States — History
2. Baseball — Social Aspects — United States
3. Baseball — Philosophy — United States
4. Baseball — Players — United States

I. Title
ISBN 1-880876-60-4

For information address: Diamond Library.
Published by Diamond Library, a division of Diamond Analytics
Corporation, with offices at:
708 North Chestnut Street, Barnesville, OH, 43713.
Telephone: 800-707-9090.

PRINTED IN THE UNITED STATES OF AMERICA

Cover design by Digital Copy, LLC

ACKNOWLEDGMENTS

Professor David Stayner of Yale helped me to understand that the method employed here is properly called "qualitative research with a protocol," a fancy way of saying that I started (almost) all of these conversations by asking exactly the same question. Knowing that there is an academic and professional discipline to shape what develops from this kind of interview helped me in numerous ways, beginning with the opportunity to draw on the experience of others.

Elizabeth Ursic, who deserves credit for bringing me to David Stayner in the first place, was yet again helpful at the manuscript stage. Through a somewhat misguided effort to be helpful to the reader by organizing this material, in an early draft I attempted to group clusters of sentences from various speakers covering one topic (such as "overcoming adversity") in hope of creating a sort of conversation with diverse voices joining together. This method necessitated quite a few connecting sentences and editorial side comments to make the text flow. Elizabeth explained to me, kindly yet directly, that most readers are not much interested in what John Benson has to say, especially not in comparison to the level of interest in what Roger Clemens or Frank Robinson has to say. So the book ended up going back to the simplest and clearest presentation of each person's ideas.

Bill Gray, James Benson, Helene Pollock, David Male, and Rosa Packard are prominent among those who looked at early drafts and made helpful comments and suggestions. Morrie Ross was both a source of inspiration at the most important times and an influence on content and format. Above all, I am grateful to all of the interviewees who gave me their time and attention.

John Benson

INTRODUCTION

Dictionaries offer a variety of meanings for "wisdom." Every synonym fails in some aspect, and every explanation grows ponderous before it is complete enough to be useful. The nature of wisdom is that it resists packaging for easy handling. It is an elusive entity.

One concept of wisdom is knowledge: information and facts. The problem with a vast accumulation of knowledge is that it leads to an illusion of sufficiency. There is no quantity of factual knowledge that can add up to wisdom. Knowledge is a part of wisdom. Pursuit of knowledge is a wise course of action. But wisdom is not some information about something.

Another concept of wisdom is judgment: discernment, logic, reasoning, sense, or even common sense. In this concept, wisdom is an aptitude or ability, something like intelligence. One obvious problem in connecting wisdom with intelligence is that some of the brightest ideas and best minds in history have been used for dark and destructive purposes.

Although there are competing definitions, and even arguments when one person's wisdom is another's folly, everyone seems to agree that wisdom is essentially good. Wisdom has no opponents. No one is even neutral about the idea of wisdom. And unlike political theories, philosophies, and religions, no one has ever gone to war for or against wisdom.

As a starting point, wisdom might be defined as the capability to think and act well in all circumstances. Wisdom includes a set of attitudes and a disposition of mind and character, resisting any kind of formulaic codification. In practice wisdom manifests itself mainly in the long term, and wisdom typically endows humans gradually and without any point of completion. There is no last word.

"Next to religion, baseball has furnished a greater influence on American life than any other institution." Since Herbert Hoover made that observation, we may wonder if religion has lost some influence while baseball has held its own or even gained some. Can we attain wisdom by watching and pondering baseball? The people who play the game for a living, teach it, or manage others in these pursuits, are all quite certain the answer is: yes. The Bible tells us that we can grow wise by studying ants. While that idea may be valid and useful, most of us would rather learn about life from baseball.

The object of the game is to leave home successfully and then return home safely. Baseball is in tune with the seasons. Baseball respects nature, including weather and topography. The size and shape of the field refuse to be standardized. The game will not yield to any clock or other human invention, although rain can bring the game to an end.

Baseball endures. There will always be a tomorrow and a next year. Through wars, earthquakes and other natural disasters, stock market crashes and other financial panics, economic depressions, and constitutional crises, organized baseball continues.

The influence of baseball can be sensed in the extent to which the baseball culture influences its observers' language and thinking. The beginning is right off the bat. Success is a hit. Big success is a home run, and the biggest success is a grand slam. Failure is when we don't get to first base. Total failure is when we strike out. A reasonable estimate is in the ballpark. An unreasonable stance is off base. An absurd attitude is out in left field. A surprising difficulty is when someone throws you a curve. Being in a difficult situation is having two strikes against you. A diligent worker will touch base frequently and will touch all bases before going home.

The thesis here is that the baseball culture is rich in ideas, images and thought forms that can impart wisdom. The challenge is to take what has been oral tradition for a hundred years, and begin reducing it to writing. The result is a form of what might be called wisdom literature.

Wisdom literature is about as old as writing itself. Every culture, for as long as it can remember, has been engaged in a methodical effort to document the ways to good living. Every civilization has produced writings to engender success and happiness in everyday life and to develop fathomable explanations for unexpected bad outcomes.

In most traditions, including the Judeo-Christian stream, writing about wisdom went through definite stages. Oversimplified, the first stage was to offer advice to young people and to those who would exercise leadership. In this early stage, wisdom literature tended to focus on specific behaviors with clear sets of do's and don'ts. Such writings often included promises of good outcomes for those who followed instructions, and warnings of bad outcomes for those who violated the behavioral guidelines.

Increasingly sophisticated understandings soon became necessary, because the world seldom functions as a mechanism. Although certain patterns of behavior tend to yield certain patterns of results, there can be extreme exceptions to the generalizations about good and bad behaviors. While some people break all the rules and seem to enjoy health and prosperity, others live within every known guideline and yet seem to suffer endless calamities.

One way of illuminating the path to wisdom without indulging in simplistic, if-then mechanistic thinking is to utilize biography, storytelling, and role models. Real events in the lives of real people offer excellent proving grounds for anyone considering how to proceed in a particular situation. Stories can illustrate the whole spectrum of good behavior and bad behavior, clear thinking and confused muddling, virtuous attitudes and the worst prejudices.

Choice of language is another way to allow for gradations of wisdom and to allow room for mystery. A simple shift from nouns and verbs toward adjectives and adverbs can nudge thinking away from long and complicated mechanistic behavioral codes and point people to a basic set of attitudes and dispositions. The result is less formulaic, less focused on outward appearances, and more focused on the subject's inward disposition.

Wisdom literature long ago took two major steps toward sophistication. The first was the recognition that certain profound truths cannot be grasped quickly and easily. People with more experience and maturity tend to possess more wisdom than do the young and inexperienced. Teachers and teachings can only do so much to impart wisdom.

The second major step in the development of the classic wisdom traditions centered on the admission that pure mystery is always in the equation. At some point the sapiential enterprise must come to grips with the finitude of the human mind. Not everything can always be understandable and explainable. In Anglo-American culture, Enlightenment metaphysics and epistemology focused on the simple reality that our brains are just not big enough to understand and explain how we know what we know, much less comprehend the reasons why we don't know what we don't know. We must eventually confess that some element of mystery seems always to be with us.

Every culture, including baseball, has names for the unexplainable. Bart Giamatti named the mystery element in baseball "Dame Mutability." More commonly baseball people speak of "fate" or what is "just meant to happen." Game after game and year after year, we come to see more clearly the boundaries of what is knowable, and we can perceive the contours of what is unknowable. This collection of interviews engages both.

An assertion that Roger Clemens is the greatest pitcher of the modern era could begin with the fact that Clemens is the only pitcher ever to win the Cy Young Award seven times. Even more remarkable is the span from his first in 1986 to his seventh in 2004. No one else has been close to achieving such a high level of success over such a long time. Randy Johnson's five Cy Young Awards came in an eight-year period. Greg Maddux won his four Cy Young Awards in four consecutive seasons. In 2003 Clemens became the active career leader in wins, innings, starts, complete games, shutouts, and most other objective measures of longevity with success.

One hot afternoon in the summer of 1992, hours before game time, I sat in the shade of the Yankee dugout, chatting idly with Tony Kubek and staring out upon a sunny field where almost nothing was happening. It was long before team workouts would begin. Every few minutes a solitary jogger would chug past us. It was Clemens, after whose fifth or sixth lap around the perimeter of the field, Kubek turned his head slightly toward Clemens and commented, "He's very intense, driven. He's on a different level."

My father passed away real young. My mother raised six of us. We had to work together to survive. I learned that lesson well before I started playing baseball. My mother and grandmother taught me how to respect and have passion for what you do, and work together for one common goal.

I know more than a handful of guys that were better talented than I was, that never made it. I don't know why, if they got off track, or maybe they were satisfied just being a major league ballplayer. They were able to do that, get their signing bonus, and get their car, and say that they were a major league ballplayer.

I was almost the opposite. I was giving my mom a shout when I was riding six hours on a bus [in the minor leagues]. That wasn't our idea, being satisfied like that. Certain guys are going to make it to the major leagues, and they're going to make a great living. If that's what strokes you as a young player, then I'm going to stress that point for them: you're going to make a lot of money, so you take care of yourself for a long time. You stress those points.

Roger Clemens

Once you've made it, and you know it, you expect to be here for a long while. Then you start looking at other priorities, as far as winning and championships. You take what was maybe a hobby, or something that you enjoyed doing, and it becomes a career. It's become a career for me.

I learn every day what to do about the essentials of making adjustments, in my nineteenth year, in my twentieth year. So I've learned, and I continue to learn. I go back right to the fundamentals. I start over in January. I run by the local high school and get those kids, and we start the basics. I just learned from the beginning: you just continue to try and improve.

As far as anything it taught me about life, I was taught so much by my mother and grandmother about how to succeed and how to be able to handle success. I was taught a lot of qualities. And a lot of qualities I was given by just observing. That's how I've done well in this game. I've made adjustments. So, it's the same thing: make adjustments, continue to improve.

Roger Clemens

I know more than a handful of guys that were better talented than I was, that never made it.

Roger Clemens

I'm a good golfer. I play with the pro guys, and I observe and I watch. It's a challenge for me. I have golfing buddies that go out there and play to make the cut. They play real easy Thursday and Friday, get to the weekend, and make the cut. There's nothing wrong with that; they're playing to make a living. And there are guys in this game that do the same thing.

There are other guys that I've played with, I won't mention names, but they're in the top five of the PGA all the time, and when they put it in the ground Thursday, they're playing to win the tournament. That's a whole different game. They know they're going to get their money. They're playing to win. Their focus is on that. It's just your approach and your focus on what you're looking to do.

This game is still a challenge for me. Life and family is still a challenge every day. With four boys and juggling that team: I have a team there, and I have a team here. I have to juggle the two, and I have to give discipline and respect to both.

They say life begins after 40, and I'm finding out.

Roger Clemens

I never want to be satisfied or complacent because then, like I said, if you're going to let people know that, you're a loser. That's in any field. That's in any job. You have that in anything that you're doing.

You really want to enjoy what you do and love what you do, or it's more than work. We treat our job very seriously even though it's a game, and we try to bring enjoyment. I want people to be excited about what I do whether I'm striking a guy out or whatever is going on. In a visiting ballpark, you want them to dislike you and root against you. In the long run they appreciate what you do and what you bring to the game.

Roger Clemens

Beginning with a 1991 team that went from worst to first, Bobby Cox led the Atlanta Braves to 14 championships in 15 seasons (finishing second in the strike-shortened 1994 season). During this era Cox and the Braves have won more games than any other major league team. Cox and Joe McCarthy are the only two managers ever to guide their teams to 100 or more wins in a season six times. For total career margin of wins exceeding losses, Cox is ahead of every manager in history except McCarthy and John McGraw. Cox has been named Manager of the Year by *The Sporting News* seven times; no other manager has won this distinction more than three times since 1936 when balloting began.

When I found Cox to get this interview, he was sitting alone in his dugout. It was early September. I asked what he was thinking about. He said he was planning his postseason roster, going over again and again possible combinations of players that added up to a total of 25 names. It seems likely that Cox has spent more time than any other manager in baseball history, thinking about postseason rosters, perhaps by a factor of ten over the runner-up.

The more you're around people, the more you mature and learn about yourself. The more you grow up, the smarter you become. You learn which people to trust and which people not to trust, which people to follow, and which people not to follow. It's like any other line of work. The learning process is exactly the same.

In baseball you get the opportunity to meet so many different people. It's one of the occupations where you actually travel from city to city. You're in airports. You're in ballparks, and at charity events. You're promoting events during the winter and constantly meeting people. You learn how to be a social person.

Observation plays a huge part in a lot of people's development, in any form of work, especially in baseball: watching, learning, watching some more, experimenting, and listening. Watching and listening: "Keep your eyes and ears open." That's an expression that's old, that is so true.

The number one key to winning is having good players. Make sure you always get good

Bobby Cox

The number one key to winning is having good players.

Bobby Cox

players on your team.

There is a lot of luck in life, being at the right place at the right time. Everything goes through cycles. When the market is up, a lot of people have success in it. Some people get in at high numbers, and the market drops. They don't have success. Those people who bought low and sold high are no smarter than the ones that bought high and sold low. The ball didn't bounce their way at the right time. I can contend that there is a lot of luck throughout life.

Bobby Cox

When he retired in 2005, John Franco was the game's oldest pitcher (44) and the active leader in career appearances among all pitchers. Franco, the eighth pitcher in baseball history to appear in over a thousand games, is most noted for his accomplishments as an ace reliever. He holds the all-time National League record for career saves, the all-time major league record for career saves by a lefthanded pitcher, and has the all-time second highest career total for major league saves (behind Lee Smith). At age 43 in 2004, Franco retired 26 consecutive lefthanded batters in May and June.

John Franco

Baseball teaches you how to communicate with people, people from all different ethnic backgrounds: Spanish, Black, Puerto Rican. It teaches you there are different cultures. It teaches you to enjoy life. We have been blessed with a gift to play this game and have our families enjoy life in a way our parents didn't. It teaches you how to appreciate what you have, really.

Sometimes you learn more just by observing and keeping your mouth shut. You learn how to handle adversity, how to handle success, see what you're dealing with at that time in life, and how to be a good judge of people. You observe how people handle adversity, how people handle tough times. In good times, and then in bad times they don't want to know anybody, and you have to walk on egg shells to get things across.

Sometimes you learn more just by observing and keeping your mouth shut.

John Franco

Tom Hume, when I was with Cincinnati when I first came up, said: don't get too high and don't get too low. Just stay on an even keel. You are going to have good days and bad days. Always say to yourself, you are going to have more good days than bad days. I try to stay even.

As soon as you get on top of that hill, somebody's going to be there to try to knock you off.

John Franco

Tom Glavine is a nine-time All-Star and two-time Cy Young Award winner. He has won 20 or more games in a season five times and has led the National League in wins five times. At the beginning of the 2006 season he had more career wins than any active pitcher except Roger Clemens and Greg Maddux, and more career shutouts than anyone except Clemens, Maddux, and Randy Johnson. Glavine has been to the World Series five times and has a 2.16 ERA in 58 innings of World Series competition.

Tom Glavine

Things that come to mind are communication skills, teamwork skills, and commitment. You have to have all those things to be a successful team. As much as you're responsible for yourself individually, you're part of a bigger picture, and the better you are able to communicate and compete and work together with your teammates, then the more valuable you're going to be. I think that's true in a lot of other situations in life as well.

There are things you obviously need to communicate on the field. You have to, on certain plays, be able to communicate who's going to do what, who's going to be where. Take charge of the situation. I think that you have to be able, off the field, to communicate as a group, what your goals are, what you need to do to go about achieving those goals. If somebody is not holding up their end of the bargain, you have to be able to communicate to them that you expect more of them, those kinds of things.

So much of what goes on, on the baseball field, requires either verbal communication or just a kind of a physical presence type of communication. Sometimes even though

Tom Glavine

something is not verbally spoken, there's still a gesture, an understanding that somebody is going to be somewhere, in a certain situation. You have to be able to communicate that to your teammates and know that it's going to happen.

Generally you want players to be in a position where they know what's going to happen before the play actually takes place. Again, so much of that is having been in situations before, and you talk about it. You talk about why it went right or why it went wrong, so when you're in that position again, the next time you eliminate that uncertainty. You know what's going to happen. You anticipate the play before it happens. Not only have you anticipated the play, everybody around you knows what is expected of them.

Tom Glavine

One of the most respected and experienced executives in baseball, Roland Hemond rejoined the Chicago White Sox as executive advisor to General Manager Ken Williams after the 2000 season. He has 56 years of professional baseball experience, including 23 seasons as a general manager with the White Sox (1971-85) and Baltimore Orioles (1988-95) and five seasons as a senior executive vice president with the Arizona Diamondbacks (1996-2000). Hemond is a three-time winner of Major League Baseball's Executive of the Year award, 1972, 1983 and 1989. The 1972 White Sox, featuring Hemond acquisition Dick Allen and manager Chuck Tanner, went 87-67 for the franchise's first winning record in five seasons. The 1983 club went 99-63 and won the American League West Division title by 20 games, then a record for largest winning margin. While with Baltimore in 1989, Hemond was tabbed Executive of the Year for the third time after the Orioles improved 32.5 games from the previous season. In January 2003, Jerry Reinsdorf and the Chicago White Sox announced the creation of the Roland Hemond Award in honor of those who are dedicated to bettering the lives of others through extraordinary personal sacrifice.

Baseball teaches you to be courageous, overcome adversity, be positive, appreciate the good times, and recognize when things are not going well, think how happy we will be when it goes well again, so that you keep a positive outlook. Take the game seriously, but don't take yourself seriously.

Many times pitchers are better pitchers after they have had arm problems. Early on they rely on arm strength and power pitches, and just rear back and throw, and they are not really pitchers. They are simply throwers. They may find out that they may throw hard, but the hitters hit them hard, too. They haven't really harnessed their equipment, and sometimes when they've had an ailment, then they recognize that change of speeds will be necessary, and not just throwing strikes but quality strikes, and add some deceptions in their deliveries. It teaches them that it was great that they had the arm strength to begin with, and that's why, early in their careers, we like pitchers with good arm strength recognizing that they can learn to pitch. Often times after they have had adversity, then they take better care of that equipment, that arm of theirs.

Roland Hemond

Sometimes they are careless. It will be cold outside. They won't put their jacket on after they stop pitching and they are still perspiring. In the old days they used to jump on that: "Get the jacket on. Get the jacket!" Today you don't see them do that as much, but nevertheless, to last, they have got to protect that treasure.

In this day and age, with improved mechanics, and fine coaches, some people do add [velocity] to their fastball.

In many cases the salaries of young players now are such that they don't have to find other jobs in the wintertime, so that they can be conditioning themselves and throw on the side, so when they show up at spring training they are basically in real fine shape. In the old days they had to get employment that didn't pay well, and they would get out of shape, and then they would have to use spring training as a method of getting ready for opening day.

As human beings, we strive and we work hard to survive, so there is a danger, when you become financially secure, that you may not

Roland Hemond

push yourself as hard, due to the fact that now you feel secure. It is a shame when people fall for that, because they have a chance to continue to have a great career, and not cast it away by personal satisfaction of the finances. Roger Clemens is a great example of having a lengthy Hall-of-Fame career due to his devotion towards physical conditioning even being financially secure.

There is life after the game, too, so that you want to be prepared to make contributions in various ways. That is the reward that you do have, if you are able to help others because of your experiences. Also, having been a player, when there is a forum for good causes, other people may wish to participate in it.

I encourage players to continue to pursue their education and get their college degree. With the University of Phoenix, they have on-line programs, and players can utilize the down time that they have on buses, planes or hotels, much better, to take some on-line courses toward getting their college degrees. We see so many players with three years of college, and then they fail to go back to get their degree. Later they are not even able to

Roland Hemond

land a high school coaching job or a college coaching job, because they don't have a college degree. People see they don't have a degree, so even if they wanted to participate in that manner, and they have all that knowledge, they can't get that fulfillment. And then if they did have their college degree, they are more attractive to various corporations, and other industries, because you might be through as a player at 40, but then live to be 75 or 80. There is a lot of time there when they could fulfill their lives and also have a better family situation, by the fact that they could show their own children the value of education.

Some are bored, because they have nothing to stimulate their intelligence as well as their fulfillment. Also, as a ballplayer there are times when, mentally, you should get away from the game. And you do if you are working on something towards your education. Tony LaRussa is a fine example. It took him twelve years of offseason study, but he attained a law degree. He passed the bar, the very first time he took the exam. Jim Snyder, who is White Sox director of minor league instruction, went to college eight off-seasons to get his degree. But now, with on-line services, it is so much easier. It would take far less time to get a degree.

Every day should be a learning process. Even if you are in the game like I have been, now this is my 55th season, I am still learning, and I wish I could start over, because I see the technology that's involved, and the growth of the game, the globalization of it, the value of various languages. These are exciting times, and the game keeps growing in popularity on a global basis. I've seen it from being with the Boston Braves, then in Milwaukee, and then two expansion clubs, the Angels when they got underway, and also the Arizona Diamondbacks. It has been very exciting for me, the evolution of each decade, and its growth has been fabulous.

I joined the California Angels three weeks after they had been awarded the franchise, as their farm and scouting director; I wasn't involved in the process of selection of players from the other teams. But then with the Diamondbacks, that was very exciting because we had two years to prepare. For our club to win a hundred games in its second

Roland Hemond

year of operation, and then win a world championship the fourth year, that was very exciting, although I left after the conclusion of the 2000 season, to rejoin the White Sox. It was gratifying to see the Diamondbacks beat the New York Yankees to win the world championship, for everybody connected with the club.

[Tell young players] just be so grateful that you are wearing a professional baseball uniform. There are so many youngsters throughout the world, hoping and praying and desiring, and putting all sorts of efforts towards the opportunity, and be faithful to the scouts who have discovered you and who have turned in favorable reports. And I would say: mention the names of the scouts who made it possible for you to be in professional baseball. And take advantage of the tremendous instruction that you receive at the professional level, and also all the facilities that are provided for you. This is a tremendous time to be a baseball player.

If they would study the history of the game, they would better realize how fortunate they really are. They are so well compensated now,

Roland Hemond

*Absorb the knowledge that is
provided for you, and always
remember who helped you.*

Roland Hemond

31

and the conditions are so good. They can't compare, because they accept what is. We have six and a half fields plus the major league field for spring training. Now I go back to Waycross, Georgia, and they were sleeping in the barracks, and the air was blowing through the barracks. Now, they stay at nice hotels, get provided good meals, proper nutrition, and excellent facilities. In the early days, there would be a minor league manager. Also he drove the bus, and he was the instructor at all the positions. Now each club in the minor leagues has a pitching coach and hitting coach to go along with the manager. Then roving pitching coaches, and hitting coaches, and baserunning coaches, come in to help. Infield coaches come in to help them, and outfield coaches. So absorb the knowledge that is provided for you, and always remember who helped you. When you are interviewed, you should mention names of people who have helped you on the path to success.

It is a difficult adjustment when they are through as a player, at the end of their career. But if they have a college degree, then they may be able to have a more normal life. They *are now in the real world and fending for themselves.*

A player should stay out of the game for a year or two after the end of his career, and experience the real world. Then he's better prepared to get back into the game. Many times they are looking forward to having more time with their family, and spend a summer with them. But then within a short period of time, maybe 12 to 24 months, they get the itch to come back and do something in the game. They miss the camaraderie, the laughs, and people staying together through September or October. Basically it is almost like living aboard ship with the same people. But then we all look forward to getting back to spring training, because we miss these baseball friends.

Sometimes you get the job with an organization, because they recognize that you have overcome adversity in the past. With the Boston Braves, we drew only 281,000 people in 1952. The next year in Milwaukee things went real well. Some of the players who had been in the service during the Korean crisis came back. We went from a seventh

Roland Hemond

place club in an eight-team league, to a second place club, drew well, and became a great club.

When I joined the Baltimore Orioles, it was November 1987. We lost our first 21 games in 1988 setting an all-time record for losses at the beginning of a season. So I used to say to myself I probably wouldn't have this job, if things were going real well in Baltimore at that time. So you give yourself a motivational message. Think how happy we will be when it gets better. The next year, we improved by 32 and a half games, and we weren't eliminated from the Eastern Division title until the next to last day of the season, in Toronto. I have often said that Frank Robinson did one of the greatest managerial jobs that I have ever witnessed, with that turnaround year. And our fans responded very well.

We finally won a game in Chicago. Then we lost two more. So we were 1-23, and when we came back to Baltimore, there were 50,402 fans there to greet the club, giving us a standing ovation. And as I was walking off the field, someone hollered out at me, "Roland,

Roland Hemond

you're doing a great job!" And I thought, boy, this is a great place to be. The next year, unfortunately, our owner, Edward Bennett Williams, who was very ill, did not live to see the turnaround in the following year. But the night we came back and had the 50,402 fans, that was a great display, in the history of sports, of fan loyalty, for which we were so grateful. That night, Edward Bennett Williams signed the agreement, with Governor Donald Schaefer of Maryland, for the building of beautiful Oriole Park at Camden Yards. And there were great moments there, with Cal Ripken surpassing Lou Gehrig's record. You have moments that you treasure. You derive the same happiness talking about it, as when it took place.

That turnaround was a combination. There were a lot of young players on the club, and some of them were graduates of our Rochester club. The previous year they had won the Governors' Cup, the International League Championship, under Johnny Oates, and John had prepared those players very well to handle the major league scene, namely Steve Finley, Brady Anderson, Bob Milacki, Pete Harnsich. They jelled as a young team.

Roland Hemond

Some veterans also played a role. It was a combination. They played so well: Phil Bradley, Joe Orsulak. It seemed that every night they were on Sports Center as outfielders, making one play after another. If they left their feet, they caught the ball. And with Cal Ripken's leadership, it was a tremendous year.

This past 2005 season, I experienced the highlight point of my career as a member of the Chicago White Sox 2005 World Series Championship. We all rejoiced that White Sox fans all over the world could celebrate this phenomenal accomplishment.

Orel Hershiser pitched 18 years in the major leagues, mainly with the Dodgers. He was a three-time All-Star. In 1988 he won the Cy Young award and was the World Series Most Valuable Player. Hershiser holds the all-time record for consecutive scoreless innings pitched. After his playing career, he served as pitching coach for the Texas Rangers, and in 2006 he joined the ESPN broadcast team as a studio analyst.

Orel Hershiser

I learned that whether you win or whether you lose, you still get a root beer, and you can get a hot dog if you're hungry. I thought that was pretty cool. I learned that Dad had a lot of fun being on a ball field with me. So, that made it a cool place to go. And it was a lot of fun to do something with my dad early on, because he was a traveling salesman.

When there was a little league game I could see him coming out of the car, pulling his tie off, and rolling up his sleeves and running towards the field to get to the game on time, to help umpire, or coach, or sit in the stands and root me on. It was just always around, just love, and companionship and a fun thing to do with my dad.

As far as the big league level, I learned that celebrities are human beings, and that they put their pants on one leg at a time. If they can remember that, they can make an impact on the world. Because, I always thought when I was growing up, that the big leaguers must've gone around in glass bubbles. And how could you make sure that they didn't get food poisoning? How could you make sure that these guys that were so wonderful and

Orel Hershiser

I learned that celebrities are human beings, and that they put their pants on one leg at a time. If they can remember that, they can make an impact on the world.

Orel Hershiser

so perfect and played on this beautiful field and everybody loved? How did you make sure that they were always safe?

And then I ended up being one, and you find out that you're just regular people that happen to have a skill that other people enjoy watching. I don't think I could have learned that anywhere else.

Something I've always remembered is what an honor it is to put this uniform on. And you have to see through other people's eyes and why they think it's so special. And I remember why I thought it was so special when I was growing up, and so I continue to have that feeling.

Don Mattingly is the New York Yankees hitting coach. In his first year in that role in 2004, Mattingly led Yankee batters to an all-time franchise record 242 home runs. As a player Mattingly was the premier first baseman of his era. In a 14-year career from 1982 through 1995 he collected 2,153 hits to rank fifth all-time among Yankee players. He was a nine-time Gold Glove Award winner and has the highest career fielding percentage of any first baseman in American League history. Mattingly was the American League Most Valuable Player in 1985.

Don Mattingly

You need to learn to handle both sides of the coin. You handle losing, and you handle success. Can you handle failure? I think you learn from both. You learn how to act when something goes your way, and how to respect the people that you're competing against. And on the other side of the coin, you learn to lose with your head up because you did your best and you can always rest in that. So I think you learn from both sides of that coin.

I learned from my very first home game here at Yankee Stadium, where I had a pretty tough day, to be honest with you. I'd made an error and some things didn't go my way, but I also learned that I can handle that, and it was over, and I moved on to the next day. I learn from those mistakes. And you move onto the next day, and you can have a good career.

Most of the guys that are here have been great athletes in high school and in college. They haven't had to really struggle. But as you move up, the talent levels are very close. So the guys that compete know how to make adjustments, handle when something goes wrong, that it's still okay. You can learn from that and move forward and get better.

Don Mattingly

You need to learn to handle both sides of the coin. You handle losing, and you handle success.

Don Mattingly

I don't know anybody that gets here without getting through some adversity. There are not too many guys that just zip through the minors without having a slump or a struggle. You're going to face it coming through the minors, because the talent level starts getting closer together from A-ball and up. There are guys that stand out. But for the most part everybody there is pretty talented, so from the time they get there they have to struggle a little bit.

We're probably one organization where kids have to work a little harder because of our veteran players, and some teams seem to bring them up pretty quick.

Don Mattingly

In 2003 with the Florida Marlins, after he had taken over a team that had a losing record, Jack McKeon became the oldest manager in baseball history to win a World Series championship. Previously McKeon managed the Kansas City Royals, Oakland Athletics, San Diego Padres, and Cincinnati Reds. He was named Manager of the Year in 1999 and 2003. McKeon was vice president of baseball operations and general manager of the San Diego Padres from 1980 to 1990. As a player he was a catcher and spent ten seasons in the minor leagues. When he retired after the 2005 season, McKeon was the third oldest manager in baseball history, after Connie Mack and Casey Stengel.

Jack McKeon

Number one, I learned to have a lot of fun, to have patience, and don't let the little things bother you. After my second stint as a manager when I managed the A's, and I laid out for nine years and came back, I realized you've got to have a little more patience. And second of all, you have to overlook some little things. If you don't hear a lot of things, and you don't see a lot of things, then the little things you don't like don't disturb you.

Those little things are like whether a guy didn't have his hat on right, or whether a guy didn't dress appropriately on the plane, or a guy didn't have his socks up high enough, some of the stuff that you had years ago that would be pretty much traditional. Or a guy's hair is a little bit too long. I don't let a lot of that little stuff bother me any more. Another thing: maybe a guy, you take him out for a pitcher, and maybe he has to gripe at you, and maybe I would have challenged him years ago. Now I don't hear it. I just look the other way. Never see it. Never hear it. Don't let it bother you.

Winning games is the big picture. [In 2003] I had to keep everybody on an even keel, not get too high or not get too low. You try to stay

Jack McKeon

focused, have your players stay focused. Preach unselfishness. Preach persistence.

There is a lot of adversity in this game every day. And the strong survive. You've got to accept it. You've got to find a way to overcome the adversity. You can't let adversity overcome you. You've got to sit back. Sometimes you've got to take a giant step backwards and survey the situation and say, "How can I get out of this?" Sometimes I've got to take a giant step backwards to go two steps forward. A lot of people don't want to do that. They're set in their ways and they're not willing to take that giant step backwards.

To succeed, number one, enjoy the game. Have fun. Second, be unselfish. Twenty-five guys doing all the little things will help win a game. Leave your egos at the door, and play unselfish baseball, and everybody wins.

Unselfish baseball is, you've got a guy on second base and nobody out. Your job is to get him over to third base in scoring position so the next guy can bring him in. If you want to be an unselfish guy, you go up there and try to hit the ball to the right side and get a

Jack McKeon

Sometimes I've got to take a giant step backwards to go two steps forward. A lot of people don't want to do that. They're set in their ways and they're not willing to take that giant step backwards.

Jack McKeon

base hit or make a ground out. Anything to the right side advances him. Whether you're a left or right-hand hitter doesn't make any difference.

Some guys will do that. Eighty percent will do that. The other twenty percent, they won't have anything in mind but getting a base hit. And what happens is, ninety percent of the time, they hit a ground ball to shortstop and won't be able to get the guy over. Or they hit a line drive at somebody, and they come back to the bench and someone will say "Oh, tough luck." And I say, "Tough luck, my ass! You didn't get the job done."

Another kind of unselfish is what you have in your bench players. You may have an outfielder sitting on the bench, and you have an outfielder who's out there playing. The guy sitting has one hundred percent support of that guy who's playing, instead of sitting there and maybe saying, "Well, I ought to be playing. He's gone oh for twelve, and I should be in there."

In that team [2003] I had a bunch of guys who were the most unselfish, dedicated guys.

Jack McKeon
49

There were players on this bench that should have been playing. They deserved to be playing and had a legitimate gripe. And I would apologize to them in a club meeting and tell them, "I wish I could play you guys." And to a man, they would come to me and say: "Don't worry about it. Just keep winning."

Being unselfish is what causes you to win. And you will see. For example, if a guy's on second and a guy hits a ground ball to second base, and makes an out, gets the guy over, he'll come back to the bench, and he'll see twenty guys come over and shake his hand saying, "Nice going. You did a good job." That's the salesmanship that has to be necessary on a manager's part to sell the players on the idea that that's a worthy cause.

Jack McKeon

Tim Raines is the bench coach for the Chicago White Sox. Previously he served the White Sox as first base coach, and he has been a minor-league manager. In a major-league playing career spanning 23 years with six teams including the White Sox, Raines was an All-Star seven times, won the NL batting title once, led the National League in runs scored two times, and led the league in stolen bases four consecutive years, 1981-1984, his first four years as a player. Raines is the fifth most prolific base-stealer in history, and he has the highest all-time success rate among players with 300 or more career stolen bases. In 2001 Raines and his son, Tim Raines, Jr., became the second ever father-son combination to play in the same game.

Tim Raines

Discipline is first. To be a successful player, you have to be disciplined in what you do: how you carry yourself, on and off the field, as far as being on time, how you prepare yourself before a game, get a routine to be prepared each and every day, and always thinking, "One day at a time." In life you pretty much have to do the same thing. No matter what you have to do, you always have to prepare yourself for that day, each and every day, and they are all different. You have to get a routine to be disciplined.

There was a point in my career, my second year of pro baseball, I went through a period where I was doing the wrong things. I was hanging out all the time and doing things other than what I was supposed to do. My career almost came to an end because of it. The only good thing that came out of that was that I learned my lesson. And that is where the discipline came in. I became a person that can remember the good and the bad. That made me mature a lot more, not only as a person but as a player. It definitely helped me to learn that.

The key thing is to do it yourself. You can't

Tim Raines

rely on someone else to help you solve your problem. Too many times when people have problems, they figure someone else is going to help them solve that problem. I think when you realize that you have a problem, that is the key: you knowing that you have a problem. Nobody has to tell you that you have a problem. You have to get it fixed, and you have to get it fixed yourself.

What kept me going so long was loving the game, loving what I was doing, having fun, and being proud of what I was doing. It wasn't the money. It wasn't the fame. It wasn't the recognition. It was just the joy of playing the game and competing, and trying to be the best that I could be. And I've always felt that the only way you can do that is to be a guy who will come out every day, work hard, and see how far you can go.

I enjoyed managing and enjoy working with younger players. That is one thing that I wanted to do when I left the game, is give something back, and I felt that giving something back was to do those things, to be a manager or a coach. I wanted to continue to be a great player, but after that,

Tim Raines

to be in the game. Not only to be a great player, but hopefully, one day they can say I was a great coach.

I am learning how to be a teacher. I was learning that toward the end of my career. I wasn't an everyday player the last two or three years. I was like a player-coach anyway. That got me ready to make the transition. I was a player, but I also felt like I was a coach as well. I felt like I was teaching more than I was playing. I got a kick out of that, because I got an opportunity to give those kids some of the knowledge that I gained over 23 years.

You have to want to be that kind of person to be a coach. There are a lot of people who have played the game, who wouldn't want to do that. They wouldn't want to have to tell a guy how to play the game. They expect those guys already in the game, and you will find, even though you've got major league players at this level, there is still a lot for them to learn. That's what I like about the game.

I was a student of the game when I played. No matter how much experience I had, every day I still felt like there is something that I can learn. Even now that I'm not playing, it's the same. I come out here every day. There will always be something that happens in a ballgame that you have never seen before. You have got to make sure you focus on what's going on.

That's what is good about baseball. Baseball is the one sport that can change from one play to the next, change the whole game around. In basketball one shot can change the score by so much. But in baseball one pitch can change the whole game. Or one hit. Or one fielding error. There could be two outs, and a guy gets on by an error, and the game could have been almost over, and in just one swing of the bat you could win or lose the ballgame.

In football you run out of time. In basketball you can run out of time. Baseball is the only sport where you can't run out of time.

Tim Raines

Frank Robinson is manager of the Washington Nationals. Previously he managed the Cleveland Indians, San Francisco Giants, Baltimore Orioles, and the Montreal Expos, the franchise that became the Nationals. When he began his managerial career with the Indians in 1975, Robinson was the first African-American manager in major league history. Robinson was the American League Manager of the Year in 1989 with the Orioles. As a player he was one of the all-time greats, a 12-time All-Star. In 1956 he was National League Rookie of the Year and set a record for most home runs by a rookie. He was the Most Valuable Player of the National League in 1961 and Most Valuable Player of the American League in 1966, making him the first player ever chosen to be MVP in both leagues. Robinson was elected to the Hall of Fame in 1982, his first year of eligibility, with votes on over 89% of all ballots. He was awarded the U.S. Presidential Medal of Freedom in 2005.

Frank Robinson

Number one is: although you try as hard as you can, and you want to be as successful as you can be, you can't always be as successful as you want to be. And I found out, winning is not everything. Sometimes you can really learn more and be more of a better person when you lose. It's how you lose, how you take that loss, how you build from that loss or disappointment. You can come back from that loss and be a better person for that.

The other big thing is learning how to deal and work with people of all personalities, and learning teamwork. This game is a team game played by individuals of all personalities.

There is individual responsibility, but you always have to have the team thoughts, what's best for the team, in your mind. As you play on the bases, in the field, whatever you are doing, you will have other people that depend on you.

Always put the team first, and individual accomplishments second. Team success is more important than any individual success. And I think that carries over into your life, when you leave the ballpark.

Frank Robinson

Sometimes you can really learn more and be more of a better person when you lose. It's how you lose, how you take that loss, how you build from that loss or disappointment. You can come back from that loss and be a better person for that.

Frank Robinson

In society, it's always better if you give, than if you receive, because if you do give, then I think good things happen for you and to you. If someone is always taking, I don't think good things always happen.

Those are two things I learned at an early age, that have served me well over the course of my career.

I try to think of other people first, and myself second. A lot of people ask, "Why do you favor this individual?" And I say, "Because I like him, because he's a good person." That doesn't mean he has to have as much as I have, or be as wealthy as I am, or as well off as I am. I like the individual personally, not by how nice the clothes are, that he has on, or how much money he has in his pocket. I like the person.

A lot of people have done a lot of things to help me or advance my career or my place in society, but I just didn't like them as individuals, so I wasn't always receptive to what they wanted to do for me. That's what it's all about: how good a person is.

Frank Robinson

After Bobby Cox, Joe Torre, and Tony LaRussa, among all active managers Bruce Bochy has the most wins with his current club. Bochy led the San Diego Padres to the NL West title in 1996, his second year as manager, for which he won both the Baseball Writers Association of America and *The Sporting News* Manager of the Year awards. Bochy won the NL pennant and *The Sporting News* award again in 1998.

As a player, Bochy had three attributes that helped him prepare for his second career as a coach and manager. First, he was a catcher, so he had to think hard about every aspect of the game including pitcher-handling and pitch selection, defensive positioning, opponents' baserunning strategies, and every hitter's strengths and weaknesses. Second, Bochy was a backup catcher, so he got to spend extra time thinking about thinking, something that was happening in baseball for over a hundred years before it was discovered and named by educational psychologists: metacognition. Third, Bochy was not a very good player, so he had to think hard about how to get the most from his abilities and how to help a team in subtle ways. In his one and only World Series at-bat, Bochy got a hit.

Bruce Bochy

What the Game Teaches Us

It's a team effort. Everybody has to pull together in the same direction to have success. That applies in all of life. In a family, you've got to work together, and pull together. In the business world, to have a successful business, everybody has to be pulling on the same rope.

Baseball has taught me that life is competitive. You've got to compete. I don't care what you are doing. In the business world, or in baseball, you have got to have that competitive nature, and keep pushing. Working together and being competitive are the two biggest lessons.

A third one is, you are going to have adversity, and it's in all aspects of life. We have it all the time in our game. You are going to have losing streaks. You are going to have slumps and struggles. That's not what is important.
What's important is having the mental toughness to persevere and to overcome adversity.

One example to illustrate all three: Kevin Brown one time went nine innings, and then the next day, we had a starting pitcher who couldn't go. We were scrambling to get a starter, because we had used up the pen the previous few days. And he came up and said, "Hey, I can help you. I can give you some innings." I wasn't going to let him pitch, but he knew we were in trouble and

Bruce Bochy

he volunteered his services.

Another example is Ken Caminiti, who could have sat out a day in Mexico. He had food poisoning and had I.V.'s hooked up. And he talked me into letting him play. He said, "The team needs me right now." We were in a pennant race, and he went out and hit two home runs. And then we went on from there and won our division.

Brett Butler is manager of the Arizona Diamondbacks' affiliate in the California League. He has been a major league first base coach and outfield coach and an instructor in baserunning and bunting. Butler had a 17-year major league playing career, playing for five teams. He had his best years with the San Francisco Giants and Los Angeles Dodgers. He led his league in games, runs, hits, walks, singles, triples, sacrifice hits, and times on base at least one year each, and he was an All-Star.

Butler's high school coach discouraged him from attempting to play baseball in college. Nonetheless Butler did play in college and became a 23rd-round professional pick in the 1979 draft. His career was interrupted in 1996 due to throat cancer. Although reports said that he would never play again, Butler returned near the end of the season and played another successful season in 1997 before retiring. Butler won the 1996 Branch Rickey Award and Lou Gehrig Memorial Award. He is a popular motivational speaker.

Brett Butler

Hard work, dedication, a positive mental outlook, and the ability to cope with adversity in a positive way will help you be successful not only in the game of baseball but also in life.

Adversity takes you sometimes to places unknown, and you didn't really know that you could go there. Some people are able to work through it and prosper. Others have a failure, or they fail with their "success" in a way that they never really feel or realize their true potential.

I had cancer in 1996, throat cancer, and the doctor said that I would never play again. And I knew, or believed, that it didn't matter what other people said. It was my tenacity, my drive, and my determination, to prove to myself as well as to everybody else, that I could come back and play. That is what kept me going. If I had died, it would have been a different story, but they said I wouldn't play again. I lost twenty pounds. To take it into a positive realm, I asked the doctor to put a number on it. "Doc, what is it, one in a hundred, or one in a thousand?" It was one in five thousand that I would be able to play again. And my response was, "Doc, it was one in ten thousand that I would get to the big leagues, so I have already cut those odds in half. Those are pretty good odds for me." So that's the way I went about it.

Brett Butler

But in turn again, I believe that if you have had it easy your whole life, and you have got professional athletes that have been on top of the mountain for a long time, and they have never experienced adversity, and then when they finally do, they don't know how to cope with it. Then that is when you can have a fall, and it's a great fall. And a lot of times people just hit rock bottom, and they don't know how to deal with it, and that is how they get into trouble.

Believe in yourself. If you don't believe in yourself, it's not going to happen. And go out and do the best you can. If you can make it, you can be satisfied. But if you don't, you can be content, knowing that you did everything that you possibly could. But to me, if you go out there and kind of half-heartedly go through it, and you don't make it, you always have that regret. I was always afraid of regret. I didn't want any regret when I walked away from the game. I didn't want to have any regret like: maybe if I would have done this, then maybe blah, blah, blah. You don't want to have that.

I believe that there are a lot of people – and I don't care what profession you are in – and when they walk away, they have got regret of some sort, given their ability to play, like, "I wish I could have, should have ..."

Brett Butler

"Doc, what is it, one in a hundred, or one in a thousand?" It was one in five thousand that I would be able to play again. And my response was,"Doc, it was one in ten thousand that I would get to the big leagues, so I have already cut those odds in half. Those are pretty good odds for me."

Brett Butler

I was a little guy, and it was, "You will never make it. You can't make it. You're too little. You hit the ball the other way. You've got to pull the ball."

What you have to do is, one, you have got to realize what your strengths are. Two is: realize what your weaknesses are. Work on your strengths, but work more on your weaknesses. To make yourself a complete player or a complete person, one way or another, and it is in life, too, work even harder on your weaknesses. In life everyone is a complete person with strengths and weaknesses. We are drawn to our strengths. What we should do is recognize our strengths, and then be drawn to our weaknesses, to make us complete, in life or in sport, baseball or football or basketball. Then work even harder on those weaknesses.

For instance, I could bunt to third base with my eyes closed. It was harder for me to bunt to second, toward the second baseman to the right side. So [when I was practicing] I would bunt twenty or thirty or fifty to third, and two hundred to second, so that it became equal, and I was comfortable. That is where we get anxiety, too. Whether it is in the game or in life, we get anxiety from the unknown.

The unknown comes because you are not willing to take a chance. We try to teach these kids, in

Brett Butler

spring training: *You know what? Take a chance. Do some things that are different. Work on things that are going to help you, so that even if you get thrown out stealing a base on a delay, or you try to do something and get thrown out, we are not going to get mad at you. We want you to stretch yourself to see where your limits are. And then from there, if you go too far, then you know, "Well, I can't do quite that. I can back up to here." And then you know where you are. Your comfort level is there. Your anxiety level goes down, and you are able to perform at your peak.*

Even if you lose, you want to look back and know: I couldn't have done anything else. I did everything I could do. I couldn't do anything more.

If you hang around this game long enough, you see everything.

Brett Butler

David Dombrowski is president, CEO and general manager of the Detroit Tigers. Previously he was president and general manager of the Florida Marlins and was the architect of their 1997 World Series Champion team. Before the Marlins recruited him in 1991 to begin planning for their 1993 inaugural season, Dombrowski served with the Montreal Expos as director of minor league clubs, assistant to the general manager, vice president and general manager. He began his career in 1978 with the Chicago White Sox where he served as assistant general manager under Roland Hemond. Dombrowski attended Cornell University and graduated from Western Michigan University in 1978 with a degree in business administration.

David Dombrowski

The game teaches you, first of all, discipline. Discipline is a very important part of success in life but in sports in particular. You have to be very disciplined to be a quality player as you move up the ladder. And I think that that is an important learning ingredient, that helps you with life, and I think sports develops that.

Of course you have the teamwork aspect. You depend upon other people to be successful in this game. You have to take care of your own business, but you [also] have to develop the teamwork relationship, and you have to rely upon other people in that interaction.

You have to be able to deal with failure. This is a game where even the best players fail. We all talk about .300 hitters failing seven out of ten times. But it's even more than that, because there are very few players at the minor league level that start in the game and just rise on a straight line. Young players usually don't go up a straight steady line. Most of them have the ups and downs associated with the game, and I think this game really makes you cope with that; it is magnified here more, but it really represents life in general.

David Dombrowski

Players that are successful in this game have to deal with the failures that are associated with their performance on the field, with making adjustments, and then that also carries on to other facets of their life. So how do they cope with failure off the field? How do they cope with that, in their personal relationships? With their families? With their friends? With their teammates? And so, this game emphasizes the ability to cope with failure.

Steady development doesn't happen a lot. Also, you're doing it in the public eye. That is something else that you have to cope with. In other industries, not all, but a lot of other industries, your successes and failures aren't written about or covered on a daily basis. I think that it takes a special person in the reality of learning how to cope with that, because it can create more pressure on you. And you have to realize that.

I think it teaches you the discipline of taking care of your own business. Even though it does create teamwork, in that big picture, you have to worry about being disciplined, and you have to take care of the little things to be

David Dombrowski

Roland said, "David, I'm going to tell you something, and try to give you a lesson. You can't control the weather. So don't worry about it."

David Dombrowski

successful, making your adjustments. The public limelight can be very difficult.

The game has grown as we've all seen. There is so much more media coverage. It's there on a daily basis with the internet, and the sports talk shows, so you have a lot more of that than you used to have. I think that those are areas that are particular to sports and to our game.

A big lesson, and I learned it at a young age, I learned from Roland Hemond, who was the general manager of the White Sox. He taught me to only worry about what I can control. I remember the experience. It was my first year with the White Sox. I was walking with Roland, and it was raining outside. It was early in the day, and it was probably one of those times we were all tired and all that, and I said, "Gee, I think it's going to be a tough day. We've got clouds over us. It might rain." And Roland said, "David, I'm going to tell you something, and try to give you a lesson. You can't control the weather. So don't worry about it. And just remember to apply that to your life and your job, because in things you can't control, there's no sense in spending a lot of energy on worrying about them." You

David Dombrowski

73

have to stop and think about it. We have to deal with it. Is there a rain delay? Is there not a rain delay? But it's strictly beyond our control.

That lesson has helped me in all facets of my life, because a lot of times, even being president and general manager of a team, when you're involved with a lot of things, there are so many things that happen that are not in your control. So there's no sense in worrying about those particular areas. Worry about those things that you can control, or have input in.

David Dombrowski

Tim Flannery played second base, third base, and some shortstop for the Padres from 1979 to 1989. He coached and managed in the minor leagues for several years, guiding his team to the 1994 California League championship. He then held the position of third base coach for the major league team for seven years. In 2005 Flannery entered the broadcast booth. An accomplished musician, Flannery has seven CD's to his credit.

Tim Flannery

75

The same thing seems to keep being taught to me, that this game can humble you. It doesn't matter who you are. I've seen Mike Schmidt booed, all the greats.

You've got to have mental toughness. That's what I tell my son now: how the game will break you if you don't have humility. It'll humble you no matter who you are, and you always have to respect that.

There are some things that keep coming. I respect it so much, I don't like to talk about it that much: I think it's a karma thing. What goes around comes around. As soon as you make fun of another third base coach, or make fun of another ballplayer, usually the same thing happens to you and sometimes a little bit more. There is something about the game itself. You might not believe it when you start, but some years later you can at least give it a thought.

As a musician I find parallels. You better be prepared. You better be able to deal with things not always being right: the sound, the venue, the business of the music side of it. The parallels are incredible.

Tim Flannery

I think it's a karma thing. What goes around comes around. As soon as you make fun of another third base coach, or make fun of another ballplayer, usually the same thing happens to you and sometimes a little bit more.

Tim Flannery

But again, I think the key is that when you leave the stage or leave the field, knowing that you've done all that you possibly can do, and control the things you can control. Because there are so many outside things you can't control, and we let that affect us sometimes.

Terry Francona became manager of the Boston Red Sox in 2004 and promptly led the team to its first World Championship since 1918. Francona is the only manager in baseball history to win a postseason series after losing the first three games. He accomplished this comeback feat against the 2004 Yankees and then swept the Cardinals in four games in the World Series, finishing the remarkable season with eight consecutive victories. Before joining the Red Sox, Francona served as a coach for three major league teams, and he managed the Philadelphia Phillies from 1997 to 2000.

Terry Francona

Baseball is all about making adjustments and learning to mature, treating people with respect. That's baseball. That's what you learn coming up. You learn not to fire your helmet at your teammate. You learn to listen to a coach. It's like any job. You are going to have a boss, and you have to listen to him. You may agree with him or not, but you listen.

It starts early in life. Little league baseball and youth sports are fantastic for kids to learn about life. Not necessarily to become a major league player, but to learn how to treat people and how to respect, not only the game, but respect people. My daughters play softball. My sons played.

It's all about making adjustments in life. When you're an eight-year-old, you strike out and cry. You come back as a nine-year-old, you go from crying to pouting. You come back as ten or eleven-year-old, and you're starting to deal with that. That's life.

And you watch kids. You watch them at each level as they learn to mature a little bit and they handle situations better, especially failures. That's good for them. Even how they handle success, how they treat their teammates, how they treat their

Terry Francona

It's like any job.
You are going to have a boss,
and you have to listen to him.
You may agree with him or not,
but you listen.

Terry Francona

coaches. It's great for them, great experience. They don't have to become a superstar athlete to get something out of that.

Baseball is a great trainer for the coaches, too. I don't doubt that. I think what happens is, most coaches get into it because they care.

This is a job. I want to get paid. I'd like to make a lot of money, but the reason you get in is not for the money. The reason you get in is because, obviously, you like to have that impact on people. That's a big reward. Whatever your record is, though, sometimes the little things are the reward.

When you see a player take an extra base or something that he didn't do before, you see him, that he's learning. And you go home that night saying: he's getting it! And that's a great feeling, to have that impact. Teachers have a pretty big impact on kids. I mean, when you think about it as a parent, obviously, the kids spend a heck of a lot more time with their teachers and coaches than they do with their parents.

Coaches have to love the kids, see their progress. Get joy in the little things. Whether you win the game or lose, always little things are there to enjoy.

Terry Francona

Jason Giambi was the American League's Most Valuable Player in 2000 and runner-up for that award in 2001. He joined the Yankees in 2002 and distinguished himself by hitting 41 home runs, the most by any first-year Yankee since Babe Ruth in 1920. Giambi hit 41 homers again in 2003. His career took a serious downturn in 2004 when he suffered knee, hip, back, groin, and ankle injuries, and he was hospitalized with a stomach virus and intestinal infection and treated for a tumor. He missed more than half of the 2004 season and was left off the Yankees' postseason roster. In early 2005 Giambi's performance was so weak that many observers thought his career was coming to an end. In April, May, and June combined he collected only five home runs. Then in July 2005 Giambi hit 14 home runs, the most in a calendar month by any Yankee since Mickey Mantle hit 14 in July 1961. In July, August and September 2005 combined - half a season - Giambi hit 27 home runs, the highest three-month total of his career.

Jason Giambi

I've learned a lot of things: discipline, patience, and being able to interact with people. You are around a lot of people a lot of the time. It's definitely made me, because of my experience in baseball, more worldly. I've traveled to Japan, Puerto Rico and Cuba. I've traveled all around because of this game; it gave me a lot of great opportunities that I don't know if I could have taken advantage of, if I didn't play.

This game takes a lot of discipline. You go out there every single day. And it takes patience, because a lot of times this game is a game of failure. You only succeed three out of ten times. Seven times you're making an out or getting out, so you have to have some patience and some discipline; and go through the tough times, work on them, and keep working harder to get ready for the good times.

I always try to stay even. I try never to get too high or too low. Try to keep an even keel. When I first got in the big leagues, the older players would say: it's not a sprint; it's a marathon. It's not where you start; it's where you end. Some years are going to start great and end bad. Some will start bad and end

Jason Giambi

*It's not where you start;
it's where you end.
Some years are going to start
great and end bad. Some will
start bad and end great.*

Jason Giambi

great. You have to find that happy medium, so you don't have so many peaks and valleys. I learned more in the pros. Growing up and being able to play at a certain level, most of the times it seems you're always the best player. Growing up you're always good here and good there.

At this level the only thing that separates you from another guy, sometimes, is your mental capacity. It's how you handle your highs and lows. Everybody is God gifted, no doubt about it. That's the reason some have great hand/ eye coordination. Some guys can run better than others. Some guys can't. Some guys are bigger. Some guys are stronger. It seems like the guys who have the mental attitude to play at this level are the ones who succeed.

Jason Giambi

Tom Grieve became a television broadcaster for the Texas Rangers in 1995, after serving ten years as the team's vice president and general manager. Before that he had a ten-year major-league playing career. Since he was a first round draft pick out of high school in 1966, Grieve has been with the Texas Rangers organization continuously except for one year. His son Ben Grieve was the 1998 American League Rookie of the Year.

Tom Grieve

When I was five years old, my dad gave me a first baseman's mitt, the first glove I ever had, that he got me with S&H green stamps. And he taught me how to play catch. His favorite team was the Braves. He loved Warren Spahn. My favorite team was the Yankees. I loved Mickey Mantle and Whitey Ford. While we played catch he would tell me about the players and teach me about the game. So, I envisioned what it looked like, what the players looked like, and then I started listening to Mel Allen and Red Barber describe the ballpark and the monuments.

And then he took me to a game when I was nine years old. I'll never forget walking through the tunnel and looking out there. No matter what you could imagine, as a child it was bigger and more incredible than I ever imagined, the grass, the monuments, the players. And so my dream was always to become a baseball player.

Then I got the chance to become a player, and as fate would have it, the first game I ever played was at Yankee Stadium. I flew all night from Denver, got here about 11:00 in the morning. Ted Williams was our manager.

Tom Grieve

I looked at the lineup card and didn't expect to be playing. And I was playing. Fritz Peterson was pitching for the Yankees. I was in the on-deck circle and all I could think about was that I sat up there in the stands for a game one time, watching Mickey Mantle play. I thought of the players that had stood in this on-deck circle. Then when I got to home plate, I didn't even focus on Fritz Peterson. All I could think was, all the Yankee players who had stood in the same spot. Who am I to be here? I collected their baseball cards. Anyway, I got through that game. My knees were shaking.

I played my career and then had a front office career. My youngest son became a player with the Oakland A's. They came to Yankee Stadium for the playoffs several years ago, so I came to watch him. I got here early. I walked around the monuments one more time. Then I sat in the stands and watched him play his game. It wasn't similar in any way. It was an entirely different experience. When I look back, first I remember the awe that I had as a child, and then the reverence that I had as a player, and then the pride that I had as a father watching my son play.

Tom Grieve

The tie-in to the whole thing was Bob Shephard. The one thing I remembered from the first time I came here was Bob Shephard saying, "Number seven, Mickey Mantle." For some reason that stuck in my head. So when I was in the on-deck circle as a player, and went to home plate, it never occurred to me that the same guy would be there. I hear, "Number four", and Holy Cow, he's saying my name. He knows who I am! And then watching them play years later, "Ben Grieve, number 14." I was probably eight when I came here. Then I was 52. It's like 44 years later. Bob Shephard had announced my favorite players, then me as a player, and then my son as a player. I guess it's the only place that can pass that test of time.

So when I think of what baseball means to me, I think of playing catch with my father, and then becoming a player, and then seeing my son become a player. It's not only been my life, it's been a generation. Two generations.

One lesson I learned is a funny lesson, and it may only apply to me. I would have been better off as a player if I had never heard of

Tom Grieve

the New York Yankees or any of those players, because I spent two or three years feeling like I shouldn't even be here. I mean I had these guys on my baseball cards. How can I get a hit off of Sam McDowell, or Dave McNally, or Jim Palmer? I'm thinking, shucks, if I had never heard of these guys, it never would've occurred to me that I shouldn't be here. I was just as good as them. But really, I think it took away from the first couple of years, because I didn't have the feeling that I belonged. I felt like a fan, and I would be more comfortable going off and asking these guys to sign my baseball cards, than to play with them.

Looking back at it, there are simpler lessons that you learn. You have seven months when you're with these guys all day long, in the hotel, on the bus, in the planes, in the dugout, on the bench. So you learn a lot of healthy lessons about how to get along with people, and the concept that the team is more important than the individuals.

You hear other players talk about baseball, and I always was disappointed when people didn't have the same feeling for the game. I

Tom Grieve

mean they liked to play the game, but they didn't have the history of the game. When I was farm director for the Rangers, talking to the younger players, one day I was on the bench in our ballpark, and Harmon Killebrew was there with the Twins. He was an announcer with the Twins, and he walked by. Talking to one of our draft choices, there was a little bit of a generation gap, and I didn't know what to talk to him about. He didn't know what to talk to me about.

So I said, "Do you recognize that guy?"
He said, "No."
I said, "Harmon Killebrew."
"Oh."
"You ever heard of Harmon Killebrew?"
" No. Who's Harmon Killebrew?"

This guy didn't even know who Harmon Killebrew was. So Marty Scott my assistant and I threatened to come up with a curriculum on baseball appreciation for spring training for every minor league player. And all hundred players, for three nights a week, for an hour, would have to come and listen to us or whoever else we could get to teach them about an appreciation for the game and the

Tom Grieve

That's what I did with all my kids, and they let their guard down while playing catch. You get them to talk about some things. You sit at the dinner table and you ask them questions and you don't get a damn thing. Playing catch leisurely, you do.

Tom Grieve

93

history of the game. We never did it. We probably should've done it. We even threatened to have a quiz after each night and a test at the end, and prizes to the people who paid the best attention. It would include Dominican history, Puerto Rican history, and history for every nationality that we had. So it wasn't just that Sammy Sosa was going to have to learn about Babe Ruth. We never did that, but it always amazes me that these guys can play the game and not have one clue as to, especially now, who was Curt Flood, and who was Andy Messersmith. They look at you like you're crazy.

I had this awe of the game. Maybe it was just me. I don't know. Maybe it was a personal problem or a lack of confidence or whatever it might have been. But it was awe of the game. We weren't trying to teach them to be in awe of the game. We just wanted them to know who Babe Ruth was, and who Ty Cobb was, and we just wanted them to know the history and the rules. And sometimes, the guys don't even know the rules, just simple things. Where was baseball invented? Who invented it? The different theories on it, was it Abner Doubleday or Alexander Cartright?

Tom Grieve

When did they play the first night game at Wrigley Field? Just things like that.

There is nothing like a baseball game. Kids don't go out in a driveway with their fathers, shooting foul shots and talking about pro basketball. They don't, except in rare cases, go tossing a football around and talking about the NFL. But, they do play catch and talk about baseball, because it's not just one game a week.

Baseball is every single day. Something new happens, your team wins, a guy gets hurt, or your favorite player hits a home run to win a game. Mariano Rivera is hurt? Ah, shucks. There is something every day, so if your dad comes home at five o'clock every day, and you play catch with him every day, you've got something new to talk about every day. It's unique. It's a unique sport.

Some dads teach their kids how to play catch because they want them to be a major league player. Most of them realize the chances of that are one in fifty million, but you teach your kids to play catch and maybe play little league, so at least they have an appreciation.

Tom Grieve

You just want them to know about it. It's the national pastime. You don't have to be good at it. Just, here's a glove, and here's a ball. Here's how you catch it. That's what I did with all my kids, and they let their guard down while playing catch. You get them to talk about some things. You sit at the dinner table and you ask them questions and you don't get a damn thing. Playing catch leisurely, you do. That's what baseball is for me.

Tom Grieve

Ernie Harwell has over six decades of experience as a baseball writer and broadcast journalist, primarily on radio. After writing for *The Sporting News* and the Atlanta *Constitution*, Harwell got his first job in radio broadcasting in 1940. When Brooklyn Dodgers general manager Branch Rickey noticed him and wanted to obtain his contract in 1948, Harwell became the only broadcaster in baseball history ever traded for a player. Harwell spent most of his career with the Tigers, and he did national broadcasts for CBS Radio, including two All-Star games, two World Series, and the CBS Game of the Week from 1992 to 1997. Harwell is the author of several books including *Ernie Harwell: My 60 Years in Baseball*, with Tom Keegan, published by Triumph Books in 2002. During his career Harwell was noted for beginning his first broadcast of spring with a reading from the Song of Solomon, "For lo, the winter is past ..."

Ernie Harwell

A guy can have great physical ability but he can be lacking in character. In other words, if he's a pitcher he can get out there and things can bother him too much. He can't react, and his mental condition, his approach, will also affect his physical condition. He'll choke up, tense up, and he can't relax.

All the batting coaches always say, "Stay within yourself," and the pitching coaches say the same thing. "Don't overthrow. Don't overswing. Discipline yourself." And without discipline, no matter how much natural talent the guy has, he can't get the job done in the right way.

Or a guy can succeed who doesn't have great physical ability. Eddie Stanky and Pete Rose and a lot of those guys have been great examples for me of players who didn't have a whole lot of ability, but they worked hard and they dedicated themselves to what they were doing, and they didn't let anything stop them. Like Branch Rickey said about Stanky, he can't field, he can't hit a thing, can't throw, but I'd rather have him on my team than any other player because he's a team man. He's got the right attitude. And Pete Rose. Sparky

Ernie Harwell

Anderson told me that Pete would go to the batting cage and take batting practice until his hands bled. He was so intent on making the most of his abilities.

One of the saddest things for me is to see a guy with great ability let that waste away, and not capitalize on it the way Rose did and Stanky did.

God makes us all different, and you know we have to take what he gives us and make the most of it.

Most of the good managers and the coaches [who were not the most gifted players] that can relay their experience and teach well certainly appeal to players, because they can empathize with the players that make mistakes. Guys like Ted Williams and Rogers Hornsby, people like that were so good that they couldn't understand why everybody couldn't hit .380. And maybe they were a little impatient when a guy didn't do the job the way he should.

A guy that sat on the bench, a fellow like Sparky Anderson, for instance, who only had

Ernie Harwell

*God gives us certain
difficulties so we can grow,
like an oyster, you know. You
don't get a pearl with a smooth
oyster. You have got to have
some kind of a little irritation in
there, and that builds the pearl.
You have to have a little bit of
friction to makes things grow.*

Ernie Harwell

one year in the major leagues, he understands the role of the these guys. He understands their frustrations and their attitudes and their shortcomings a lot better than Hornsby or Williams would.

Life in general is not always a pleasant journey. I think the way you respond to difficulties is a character builder. I think that's Biblical, that God gives us certain difficulties so we can grow, like an oyster, you know. You don't get a pearl with a smooth oyster. You have got to have some kind of a little irritation in there, and that builds the pearl. You have to have a little bit of friction to makes things grow. And there are a lot of examples or analogies like that, but that's one of them.

And you have to take it as the Bible says, one day at a time; the day is sufficient unto itself.

Ernie Harwell

After setting most of the all-time pitching records at the University of Texas, Burt Hooton got to the major leagues quickly, and he pitched a no-hitter as a rookie. Hooton experienced a long and deep slump after his initial success at the major-league level. He considered quitting. A trade to the Dodgers helped him get a fresh start and go on to achieve rare success in championship competition.

Hooton had a 15-year major-league career, and for a decade he was one of the best pitchers in the National League. Hooton was instrumental in the Dodgers winning the pennant in 1977 and 1978 and the World Series in 1981. He pitched the series clincher against the Yankees and was the World Series Most Valuable Player. Hooton has coached at his alma mater and at the major and minor league levels with the Houston Astros organization.

Burt Hooton

Baseball is something I have enjoyed my whole life. While it isn't exactly work, and it is a game, baseball is a game of adversity. The best hitters fail usually, seven out of ten times. The best pitchers, the Hall of Fame pitchers, have lost 40% of their games, if you check their records.

It's a game where you must enjoy it first, and then it's a game of perseverance. It's a game where you have to persevere to find a way to win. I define a good major league player as one who can find a way to win, no matter what the circumstances are. If you apply that principle of perseverance in the face of adversity, to life, that is basically what life is about. You find a way to persevere, or succeed, or get ahead, no matter what circumstances are thrown your way.

It's real easy to feel sorry for yourself in life, and baseball is no different. Lots of guys fall into the rut of feeling sorry for themselves. I was no different. At any given time, I could fall into that. But the fact remains that you are still wearing a uniform. There is still a hitter you've got to get out, or a pitcher you have to hit, or a ball you have to field or have

Burt Hooton

to throw. And at times, the game is on the line.

With perseverance, it's a game of confidence, especially self-confidence. You've got to have a little ego to play the game well. I don't see any difference there, compared to a guy who's a good salesman. You've got to have a good ego to be a good salesman. And a guy who is president of a company has to believe in what he's doing and believe in himself, when selling or making something, or whatever he's doing. Writers have to believe that they are going to be good, before they can be good. It's not going to be easy every day, but you find a way to get a good story out.

The good ones, who can persevere, who can overcome adversity, time and time again, will succeed at the profession of baseball or any other profession. I learned that in the early seventies.

Baseball was always pretty easy for me as an amateur. It was easy for me in the minor leagues. But then some time after I got to the big leagues, some things didn't go real well, and it got to the point where I was thinking

Burt Hooton

I define a good major league player as one who can find a way to win, no matter what the circumstances are.

The guys who are the good ones persevere at that kind of thinking, that today is a new day, regardless what happened yesterday.

Burt Hooton

about doing something else, because I wasn't succeeding at what I love to do. But then a couple of people came across my path, helped simplify things, and turned my thinking around. What I always was, was a good competitor, and those people got that competitiveness back out of me.

To succeed in life, you have got to be a good competitor. Everybody who has ever played this game has had down times. I'm no different. I would imagine everyone who has been a writer has had a down time at some time.

Nobody has a good day every day. You have to put the whole package together, and then you can enjoy it, and it's rewarding.

Everybody has down times in baseball, and in life. The season can be like a lifetime. You can start off poorly in April and May, and everybody is on you, especially here in New York, they may boo you and say, "Get rid of the bum." They forget about the remaining four months. It's a whole season. If someone chooses to listen to all those negative things that people are saying about them, it can

Burt Hooton

become really easy to dig yourself a deep hole.

That's where believing in yourself comes in. You work at it. You determine to be better. You come to the ballpark every day thinking, "This is the day that I am going to turn things around." The guys who are the good ones persevere at that kind of thinking, that today is a new day, regardless what happened yesterday.

Burt Hooton

Derek Jeter was the Yankees' first round draft pick in 1992, Minor League Player of the Year in 1994, Rookie of the Year in 1996, and an All-Star six times from 1998 through 2004. Jeter's rookie season coincided with the Yankees' winning the World Series for the first time since 1978. In Jeter's first five seasons in New York, the Yankees won four World Series championships.

Jeter first appeared in the major leagues when three-time All-Star Tony Fernandez was injured for two weeks in May-June 1995. Although Jeter was unimpressive by most objective measures during this brief stint, he did his job with poise before being sent back to the minors. When Fernandez was healthy and ready to play again, he was installed at second base while Jeter remained at shortstop for four more games, a compliment to the 20-year-old for the way he had conducted himself. Manager Buck Showalter, when I asked him to summarize his impression of Jeter as a player, said, "What you notice first is that his parents obviously did a good job."

I think I have the greatest parents in the world. They taught me to always be humble.

Derek Jeter

Baseball teaches you about teamwork. It teaches you that you can't always win. You're going to make mistakes, and you learn from your mistakes. I think that applies to everything in life.

I think I have the greatest parents in the world. They taught me to always be humble. This is a game of failure. You fail more than you succeed, and you have to learn to deal with the failure and learn to deal with mistakes. And learn from your mistakes.

In terms of success, you have the teamwork idea, having a goal, working towards your goal, and having a good work ethic. Practice pays off.

Derek Jeter

Randy Johnson is a ten-time All-Star and five-time Cy Young Award winner. He is the number one pitcher of all time for strikeouts per inning and has more career strikeouts than anyone except Nolan Ryan and Roger Clemens. In 2004, at age 40, Johnson became the oldest pitcher ever to have a perfect game.

Randy Johnson

I learn from my mistakes. We study the hitters and situations that have come up, in which we haven't been successful, so that next time or next year, if the same situation comes up again, we can work through what we learned and capitalize on that.

Winning is usually earned.

If I've got eight losses, that doesn't mean that those are eight deserving losses. There could be a shutout, a one-nothing loss. On the other hand there have been some games that I won, that I pitched terribly, that I should have lost. And there have been a lot of games that I should have won. I can have a perfect game going, and then give up an infield hit, and that guy ends up scoring, and you look at that on tape, and he was out by half a step.

Anybody is susceptible to a breaking ball, if you pitch them accordingly, if you set it up. My strength is obviously my fastball. I can't go with my strength the whole game. I have to mix it up a little bit. A very strong fastball hitter, I could start him out with a couple of sliders, breaking balls down and out, stay away from him. Guys know that I'm a fastball

Randy Johnson
112

pitcher. You've got to change it up enough to where they are not staying on one pitch all the time.

Other guys, at the bottom of the order, I just go right at them, and stay with fastballs. Two sliders there could be a gift.

My first year, I just wanted to stake a claim in the rotation, and have my job the next year. I just wanted to be successful and be one of those up-and-coming pitchers who, quote, unquote, could maybe have an aura some day.

You like to think that you're going to have a job, but you never know. With the Expos, I was one of their up-and-coming pitchers. For a while, I was one of those, quote, unquote, untouchables. Anything can happen. And it usually does happen. When a team is in a pennant race, they have to go with what they feel will benefit their team at this time.

Any player can beat you. A game can be nothing-nothing, and somebody makes an error.

Randy Johnson

You look toward the veteran to be more of a threat than a rookie. The veteran has been in every situation before, been a clutch hitter, and has the experience, and that is why pitchers feel threatened more by a veteran player than by a rookie player. You are more under the microscope when you make an error, when you're a rookie, than you are when you're a veteran player.

Randy Johnson

Steve Karsay was a first round draft pick by the Toronto Blue Jays in 1990. He has appeared in postseason championship competition as a relief pitcher for the Cleveland Indians, Atlanta Braves, and New York Yankees.

Steve Karsay

I've learned a lot of patience through baseball, a lot of character. It teaches you to be a winner and how to accept losing and better accept defeat. You're not going to be successful in everything you do in life. You have to keep on working towards that goal of trying to be a champion, no matter what you do, whether it's baseball, being a lawyer, doctor, firefighter, or a policeman. To me it's proven to be helpful in life, to keep trying to achieve the best in whatever field you're in.

One day you could feel great and have the best day in the world, and the next day is so different. That's the way life goes. Every day is going to be different. You have to take what's thrown at you and try to make the best out of it.

We're public figures. We're on TV a lot. We get noticed because people like to come out and watch our profession. And it does get noticed more if we have a bad day, because it's publicized. Everybody in certain work knows that if you're not having a good day it reflects in certain ways.

To be in the major leagues, overcoming

Steve Karsay

adversity with publicity is something you have to be able to do. There's no question about that. You have to handle it day in and day out, and be consistent at what you do. Your play has to be consistent on and off the field. You're a role model, and you're noticed wherever you go in the city that you play. You're very recognizable. It's a job. It's work, and it's something that I enjoy.

Steve Karsay

Gene Lamont is the third base coach for the Detroit Tigers. He has served as a coach for several teams and has 17 years experience as a manager, four with the Chicago White Sox (1992-1995), four with the Pittsburgh Pirates (1997-2000), and nine years managing in the minor leagues. Lamont was American League Manager of the Year in 1993. As a player he was a first round draft pick in 1965 and appeared in the major leagues as a backup catcher from 1970 to 1975.

Gene Lamont

One thing I learned is the real meaning of being on time. I remember, when I first signed, I was eighteen, in the Florida State League at Daytona. One day they wanted extra batting practice. We were supposed to be there at nine o'clock, and I got there about a quarter to nine. Our manager just tore into me, saying I was late. And I kept saying I wasn't really. Late was nine. From then on, I've always been very punctual.

I don't know that I wasn't, before that. I was eighteen years old and didn't really think about it. Ever since then, along those lines, I've been more aware, and not just in baseball. In baseball a lot of things are run on a time clock. They start at a certain time, after drills that are run on a certain time, what time you do this and what time you do that.

And soon, you play so many games, I learned you are not going to win every game. While you want to win every game, you've got to learn how to not let every loss affect you, so that you don't let yesterday's loss start off the next day.

Gene Lamont

One day they wanted extra batting practice. We were supposed to be there at nine o'clock, and I got there about a quarter to nine. Our manager just tore into me, saying I was late. And I kept saying I wasn't really. Late was nine. From then on, I've always been very punctual.

Gene Lamont

You have to rebound when bad things happen. If things don't go good one day, you can't start off the next day like it's going to be another bad day. You have to rebound when bad things happen, and a lot of bad things happen. You can carry over that lesson into everyday life.

Gene Lamont

Davey Lopes is the first base coach for the Washington Nationals. He was manager of the Milwaukee Brewers in 2000 and 2001 and part of 2002, and he was on the coaching staff of the San Diego Padres for eight years. A four-time All-Star second baseman with the Los Angeles Dodgers, Lopes played for four Dodger pennant-winning teams: 1974, 1977, 1978, and 1981. He also appeared in postseason championship competition with the Chicago Cubs in 1984 and the Houston Astros in 1986. Lopes led the National League in stolen bases two times.

Davey Lopes

When you're going good, everyone is on your side. When things go bad, you find out who your true friends are. It happens a lot in athletics.

You have to realize, baseball is a big business. That doesn't always register, when you're a young player. When things are going well, everybody is for you. When things go bad, people jump ship very quickly. People that you thought were your friends, are not your friends. You find out who your friends are: they are with you through good, bad, or indifferent. I found that in 1981. People all of a sudden become a little more stand-off-ish. Your phone doesn't ring as often. That's falling.

You have to be on top to fall down.

[In coaching] you are around people a lot, but you are not around them in their everyday life. When they want to come to talk to you, you can be available, but you can't ask them to come to you. You have got to be available to the guys when something's gone awry. When they come is, obviously, when they are not doing well. That's when they come. Then

Davey Lopes

123

be comforting and motivational. Whatever they have experienced in baseball, it seems so important, but in the whole scheme of life, it's not.

You do a lot of growing up, every day. I've been booed in front of fifty thousand people. I've been traded. You do a lot of growing up. From a young player, we need to develop the man. If we don't develop the man, then it's over.

Very few things happen in baseball that wouldn't happen in real life. When you go from being very popular to being not so popular, from that standpoint, things change. But with your friends, whether you are up or down doesn't change them. Then you find out who your friends are. Almost everybody looks bad at the end of their career.

Baseball can make you recognizable across the country. It is different from being a big fish in a small pond. Maybe people still remember you, if you're in the Hall of Fame.

There is publicity. If you make a mistake in baseball, it's going to be publicized. In most

Davey Lopes

From a young player, we need to develop the man. If we don't develop the man, then it's over.

Davey Lopes

125

of life, if you make a big mistake, it will be on page fifteen, or page eleven, unless it's a horrific crime, and then it gets on the front page, or the back page. A mistake in baseball gets noticed more.

Talent gives you something to work with. You might see a player who can run, throw, hit, or field a ball, and you say, "Oh, my God, this is awesome." But for winning a game or performing over a period of time, those gifts can fall short very quickly. The most talented player can be a marginal player when it comes to playing.

The guys who really succeed are the guys who do something with their talent, who work with it. A guy can be average for throwing, average for running ability and speed, and for throwing, average. Everything is average. Even for hitting talent, he can be average, and this guy can have a great career.

It's great to have the physical tools, but they don't guarantee anything. What's inside an individual is what makes the difference, and you can't measure that. There are a lot of guys like that who become great, because of

Davey Lopes

what they have inside, not their physical tools. There are lots of guys that have the great physical tools, and they don't succeed. Sometimes, because they have the great physical tools, they don't work as hard. But there are guys who are average, and they work so hard every day for a long time, they get to the Hall of Fame.

Davey Lopes

Hal McRae became the St. Louis Cardinals hitting coach before the 2005 season. Previously he was the manager of the Kansas City Royals and the Tampa Bay Devil Rays, and he served as hitting coach for the Cincinnati Reds and Philadelphia Phillies before joining the Cardinals. As a player for 19 years, McRae was among the best hitters of his era. He was a three-time All-Star and was Designated Hitter of the Year three times.

Hal McRae

Try hard. Follow your dreams. Show leadership and respect the rights of others. Play by the rules. Baseball helps you develop. It helps with your decision making. It's a wonderful learning experience for everyone to participate in sports, not just in baseball.

To work hard, prepare. Work to succeed. Work to win. Don't expect just to win. Be willing to put in the time and effort to win. Give an honest day's work for an honest day's pay.

Leave it all in the field. If you deal with situations in baseball or professional sports and you face the challenges and you don't run away, and you face the music, you have a tendency to make good decisions off the field also, because you're going to be confronted with the same types of problems. They may look different. They may sound different. But it's the same type of problem.

The problem-solving that you experienced in life is the same problem-solving that you experience as an athlete. They might look different, might sound different, might walk different, but it's the same old problem. So,

Hal McRae

if you learned problem-solving in sports, which is mainly facing up to your challenges and responsibilities, you won't shy away from similar problems in your life. So they are directly connected.

If you fail to face your problems here, you also fail to face your problems off the field. Baseball helps you develop. It helps you mature. It helps you learn your responsibilities as a human being, not only as an athlete. You learn to trust your teammates. You learn to play for your teammates. Trust in people, period.

It's a tremendous learning experience, the things you learn in baseball that are really about life. You think it's all baseball; it's not. It's life. So it's a life learning experience to participate in sports. There are a lot of great learning experiences.

That's really the purpose of sports. It's not just to entertain people. The purpose originally was designed to develop the body and the mind. That was the purpose of the thing. To develop the body and the mind, that's what athletics is all about.

Hal McRae

Mike Mussina is a five-time All-Star and ranks sixth among active pitchers for most career wins. He is also among the top ten active pitchers for career winning percentage, innings pitched, strikeouts, complete games, and shutouts. Mussina earned a degree in economics from Stanford University in 1990.

Mike Mussina

I've been a baseball player for over 25 years. I've always been a baseball player. There are a lot of things that baseball's provided: teamwork, perseverance, constant drive to improve, learning to deal with failure, learning to deal with success.

You have to deal with failure so often, that you either learn to deal with it, or you're done.

Even successful people in this game have failed a lot. A .300 hitter means failing seven out of ten times. How many times did Reggie walk up to the plate and walk back to the dugout, and never leave the batter's box? A lot.

Defining success in this game and defining failure in this game is unique. You have to deal with failure so often, that you either learn to deal with it, or you're done.

Mike Mussina

Roy Oswalt had the most wins of any pitcher in 2004-2005 combined, and he became the first pitcher to record consecutive 20-win seasons since Randy Johnson and Curt Schilling in 2001-2002. In his first five major league seasons combined, Oswalt ranked fourth among all major league pitchers for wins and fifth best for earned run average.

Roy Oswalt

When you set goals, know what's out of your control. A lot of pitchers set goals for wins, which are beyond the control of the pitcher. You can pitch seven or eight really good innings, and get no runs scored for you. Other times you give up four or five runs, and get a lot of runs scored for you. So the win is not a good goal.

I don't set long-term goals. One start at a time is the beginning. My goals are one game at a time. Then within each game, I go batter to batter. Every game I try to last six or seven or eight innings. If I pitch long into the game, that's good for the bullpen to get some rest, and then the pen can help me some other day. Early in a game, I'll usually have a feel for how it's going to go, and so I might focus on eight innings in one game, or six at some other time.

All goals have to be realistic, and within the game. Going as long as I can go in each game is one goal for me.

I try to be direct, and go right at them, one at a time. Some pitchers may try to work around a dangerous hitter. My philosophy is, the

Roy Oswalt

A lot of pitchers set goals for wins, which are beyond the control of the pitcher.

My goals are one game at a time. Then within each game, I go batter to batter.

Roy Oswalt

135

fewer men who get on base, the fewer are going to score. So I don't give in to anyone. I challenge them. I might be aware of who's on deck, and think ahead about how to pitch to that one, but that doesn't change my thinking for the one at-bat, and I try to keep my thinking always within the one inning. Thinking ahead to another inning usually doesn't help.

When you're young, it matters who sees you perform. I was a 23rd round draft pick. I went to a small high school, thirty students in my graduating class. We didn't have a baseball team until my sophomore year. There weren't a lot of scouts around, even when I did get to go to college.

Roy Oswalt

Andy Pettitte is the winner of 14 postseason championship games with the New York Yankees and the Houston Astros, placing him second all-time for postseason wins, one behind John Smoltz. Pettitte helped his teams make it to the World Series seven times in his first eleven years. Pettitte is a two-time 21-game winner and a two-time All-Star.

Andy Pettitte

Personally, where I think this game has helped me is learning to have a whole lot of humility. To tell you the truth it's a very humbling game. You can take the things that go on here and apply them to life.

When you think you have it figured out, you don't have it figured out. Off the top of my head the first thing is that it's a very humbling game. New York is a very humbling city to play this game in. It's good, I liked playing here for that reason. I like to think I'm a pretty humble person.

I think I've had fairly good success in my career. I just continue to keep striving, to work harder, to get better and better every year. It's not about:
"What have you done for me in the past?"
It's about:
"What have you done for me lately?"
That's how life is, basically, so this is a good place to learn about life situations.

Just from the get-go, obviously '99 was a real struggling season for me. They talked about getting rid of me, trading me, stuff like that. But I came back again then, realizing I was

Andy Pettitte

*When you think
you have it figured out,
you don't have it figured out.*

Andy Pettitte

doing the best that I can. The game is a business also.

It makes things a lot easier for me to handle, just because I believe that everybody has a purpose. There is a purpose for everybody's life. I believe that God is in control of my life. It makes things a lot easier for me to handle, just knowing that He is going to put me just where He wants. That's how I approach everything in my life.

Andy Pettitte

Lou Piniella has managed the New York Yankees, Cincinnati Reds, Seattle Mariners and Tampa Bay Devil Rays. In 2005 Piniella passed Earl Weaver and Clark Griffith to rank 18th all-time for most career wins as a manager, and he ranked fourth for most career wins among all active managers. Piniella has been elected American League Manager of the Year two times. He has also served as general manager of the New York Yankees and as a commentator for Fox Sports. As a player Piniella was in the major leagues for all or part of 18 years. He was the American League Rookie of the Year in 1969.

Lou Piniella

First, you have got to be competitive. You are competing against your opponents. Before that, you are competing against your own teammates, to be on the roster, to be one of the 25, and then you are competing to be on the field.

Second, you have got to get along with people. There are 25 men on every team, and they are all different. Your success depends on getting along with every one of them. You don't have to like them, but you have to get along with them and respect them. Maybe if you're a superstar, that rare, you might be able to succeed in some way by yourself. But everyone else depends on getting along with everyone to have success.

Adversity is part of what happens, and you learn from it. Before [managing Tampa Bay] I didn't know how good a win could feel. Before, I expected to win. Now I know how good it is to win a game.

Lou Piniella

Jamie Quirk is the bench coach for the Colorado Rockies. Previously he served as a coach for the Kansas City Royals and the Texas Rangers. As a player Quirk was a catcher and played for eight teams during an 18-year span in the major leagues.

Jamie Quirk

I left home at 17 years old. I got drafted right out of high school. I guess I learned how to grow up. Baseball taught me how to grow up. I had to fend for myself right off the bat, more than I think college would have taught me at that particular time. It's been a great learning experience for life in the sense that you didn't have a counselor like you would at a college. You go in there, and you have to learn all about when to eat, when not to eat, how to take care of yourself. No one is going to tell you when to go to bed. No one is telling you when to get up. You just have to get there, get it done and learn life from experiences, good and bad.

I found the right people to hang out with. There are always good and bad people wherever you go, and, luckily, I found, or tried to find, the ones that I thought were the good ones, and tried to learn from them. There were older guys in the minor leagues, and I watched what they did. Sometimes it was the wrong thing they did, but I learned from seeing the wrong thing.

I tried to surround myself with people who I thought were the good people, who were

Jamie Quirk

veterans in the minor leagues. And once I got to the major leagues I always tried to hang around with the older guys, like Paul Splittorff, when I first came up, and Marty Pattin and Bruce Dal Canton. These guys taught me the right way to do things. I learned from them and tried to pass it on.

While I didn't think I was mature, I knew that to survive you had to be. I just tried to be. I had great parents. They taught me the right things to do and not to do. I had morals. I had a conscience, and I tried to do the right things.

Obviously, I didn't always do the right thing, but I knew when I screwed up. I was born as a Catholic and went to Catholic school. It just taught me right from wrong. I knew when I was doing wrong, and I knew it immediately, and I had to change it. There was always a lot of teaching going on, not so much baseball teaching, as just maturing.

When I came up I had to learn a lot of that myself. I wanted to make sure I was doing the right thing off the field, because I figured, if I gave myself the chance, I could be good

Jamie Quirk

I tried to surround myself with good people: people with morals, people with values, people that loved the game of baseball. These people just taught me the right things.

I was never a great player, but I lasted a long time.

Jamie Quirk

in baseball, and I didn't want to ruin it by screwing up off the field.

So I tried to surround myself with good people: people with morals, people with values, people that loved the game of baseball. These people just taught me the right things. They were good people. They lived a good life. They had families, and I just watched the way they did their work and went about their business. And I knew some day, that if I had a family, I'd want to do it the same way. I was single for a long time. I wanted to give myself every opportunity to be good at this game. I didn't want to screw it up by messing up off the field.

On the field and off the field, they had a certain way they did things. Took care of their body, and went to church if they were religious people. There was a consistency. They had routines. I believe in routines. You've got to have a routine.

You've got to try to do the same kind of thing day in and day out, to improve yourself physically, mentally, bodily, all those ways. I was never a great player, but I lasted a long time.

Jamie Quirk

Paul Ricciarini is Senior Director of Player Personnel for the Houston Astros. Previously he was Houston's director of scouting. Before coming to the Astros he worked in scouting for the Reds, Blue Jays, Braves, and Mets. George Bell, Kelly Gruber, Todd Stottlemyre and Mark Wohlers are among the players Ricciarini has signed or recommended.

We have T-shirts made up with this for all the kids coming into the spring, is: "Baseball Is Life." There are so many things that correlate with real life, that go into our game deeply. There is adversity. There are peaks and valleys. There is gaining a sense of yourself. There is honesty and dishonesty. Learning how to deal with all these human traits teaches you about the game and, more importantly, what life is all about. There is a growth process. While we call it player development, what we are talking about, in essence, is a player growing not only in his skilled athletic sense, but also in the larger world of life.

Among those who succeed by growing, many of them begin as kids who languish, with ability, in the minor leagues. And then, sometimes suddenly, they begin to learn about who they are. It may be that they have over-evaluated themselves, and maybe didn't have the work ethic that is required. The thrill that I get is, when we contract in this organization, we bring in a lot of character. We teach patience. We give kids the time and patience to learn who they are. They get a sense of themselves and grow within their

Paul Ricciarini

capabilities by not trying to do too much.

Goals are what you set for yourself, realistically. Expectations are what other people impose on you. And no one in baseball, or life, ever lives up to all of everyone else's expectations. Learning that you can be a success and be yourself within your own capability is a necessary lesson. Sometimes the outside expectations might be lower than what an athlete can really achieve, so low expectations from others can make a player underachieve, if he goes by what others expect. But the hardest experience is when those expectations are too high too soon.

The annual free agent [amateur] draft is what I call The Beast. We put millions of dollars in young people's pockets, and the expectations rise so high, so fast, no one can succeed that quickly. It's a process. And there we get back to what life is. Life is a process of growth. Where I see it in the most dramatic fashion, is in the kids right of high school, and a few from colleges, who aren't quite ready for dealing with the big dollars and all the extras and intangibles that go along with the money. Young rock stars might be a good

Paul Ricciarini

Goals are what you set for yourself, realistically. Expectations are what other people impose on you. And no one in baseball, or life, ever lives up to all of everyone else's expectations.

To identify who will succeed in this organization, unequivocally, we look for character.

Paul Ricciarini

151

analogy, but in baseball we can do something with these young people. We emphasize the intangibles. We can identify talent. That's the easy part.

It is the intangibles that will allow a player to achieve and discover what his talent can mean. He might overachieve what we expected, and do it here on the big stage. To identify who will succeed, in this organization, unequivocally, we look for character.

Character is not a part of the traditional scouting report. But we can look for it and see it when it's there. There are certain traits which are obvious. Honesty is a character trait. You can identify people who are honest with themselves. And work ethic. And family background. First of all, look at where this kid is coming from. You have to assess that. See what we have to work with. See what we have to deal with. Not everybody is going to have this perfection in their background and parenthood, obviously. A lot of good kids just haven't been given enough of a chance to learn about life. Parents are usually the first and most important teachers who can make a big difference. It can go the other way, too. We

Paul Ricciarini

have to be qualified and prepared to deal with every possible situation you can think of. On stage, here at the major league level, everything is going to happen at some time.

We do more work in that area, character, than we do in identifying tools and all that kind of talk. And I am proud of that work. We talk to the family first, and then beyond. The family introduction is basically the start of the process, and we go beyond that. We will exhaust every possible way of knowing and gleaning out information on what are we dealing with here, and who are we getting. When we're investing the kind of money that we are today, we better have a pretty good idea, beyond the gray area, of who we are bringing in.

Derek Jeter is a great example of parents making a difference. I watched him when he was in high school, back in Kalamazoo, and met his parents. It was a very impressive meeting, I can tell you that. You could see that there was a lot of quality in the background, through the parents. Derek was a lucky kid, to have been able to experience that.

Paul Ricciarini

In the George Steinbrenner era of the New York Yankees, Arthur Richman has had the most influence with the least publicity. Holding only modest job titles such as senior advisor for media relations, Richman has been credited with decision-making influence extending as far as the selection of Joe Torre as manager.

Arthur Richman

The greatest thing is to win, but even if you don't win, you still could have a wonderful life, because you are surrounded by some of the finest guys in the country. I've been in the game so many years, and so many of the guys are almost like family.

My brother Milton was with United Press International for forty-two years. He was elected to baseball's Hall of Fame and got the writer's ring. When he passed away suddenly in 1986, you couldn't get into the funeral parlor. There were so many baseball people outside waiting to come to the services, including George Steinbrenner, Joe DiMaggio, and people like that.

Baseball has been my life. In my will, I put that since I was with the St. Louis Browns, that was my religion. I got a Brownie cap in 1944, when we won the only pennant in St. Louis Brown's history. I said, "I want that cap to go on my chest in the casket." And I said to my wife, "Be sure that nobody steals it before they lower the casket into the ground."

I've had a great life, and if I go bye-bye tonight,

Arthur Richman

I haven't missed a thing. I've been able to know more people than anybody in the country, because of baseball.

I've gotten very close to the White House. Even though I'm Hebrew, I got very close to the church, the Vatican, and the many Catholic Cardinals. I even got to know the Ku Klux Klan, because you couldn't help yourself. I had one of my closest friends, a guy named Ellis Kinder. He pitched for the St. Louis Browns, and he pitched for the Red Sox. He came up to the big leagues in his middle thirties and pitched until he was 45 in the big leagues. He was one of the finest pitchers I ever met in my life. The more he stayed out late at night, the better he pitched the next day. And one year he wanted me to come home to Jackson, Tennessee, where he lived. I went home with him, and we used to like to go out together. And he took me to this joint one day, and we were having a few drinks, and I said "Elly, Elly, how can you take a Jew into a Ku Klux Klan camp?" And he said "Why? It's the only place we can get a drink on a Sunday!" [Laughs.] They treated me great. They even wanted me to come back. [Laughs.] I don't think I have, though.

Arthur Richman

When you lose, you just go out more. We used to have wonderful parties. We didn't win many games, but I knew some great guys from the St. Louis Browns, and many of them came from other clubs. And then when the Browns traded them or sold them to another club like Detroit or the Red Sox or Cleveland, I would go to see them when they came into New York, and they'd introduce me to the other guys on their clubs. That's the way I got to know everyone that's been around on all the different clubs.

A victory means a lot when you're on a losing club. It's almost like a World Series game. I was with the New York Mets for 25 years. Those were 25 of the greatest years of my life. I was on three pennant winners. We won in '69. We won in '86. And in '73 we should have won. We lost in the seventh game in the World Series. But it was great years. We had the worst club in baseball in the early years, in the early '60's, when I first got started, and George Weiss hired me as the promotion director. The promotions I started with the Mets drew so many people that we outdrew every club in baseball in attendance even when we had the worst won and lost record.

Arthur Richman

And you appreciate a victory a lot more after you have lost so many games.

In my will, I said I want ten pallbearers when I pass away, and they're all baseball people, like George Brett who's my godson, and Willie Mays. I got married in his suite. He was listed as my best man on my marriage license. And I've got some great names who I don't know if they'll all make it, but I'm sure a lot of them will. I listed 25 guys. I'm not sure all of them will show up. But at least I know about eight or ten will, so I'm not concerned about it.

When I was a kid, I lived a mile away from Yankee Stadium. I didn't have a nickel for the subway. The subway was a nickel in those days. I used to walk to Yankee Stadium, and all the Yankee players would come along and not too many of them would give you autographs. But the visiting team would come up out of the subway one or two at a time, and it just so happened to be the St. Louis Browns and they said, "Why aren't you in the ballpark?" And I said, "I don't have any money. I can't go in there. It costs 65 cents, and I don't have 65 cents." And they would take me into the clubhouse, and then they started

Arthur Richman

taking me on trips. They'd hide me in an upper berth in a Pullman car, and I'd sleep on the floor in a hotel room. And they'd feed me in the hotel dining room where they could sign for me, and that's how it all got started. Now we have a reunion every year. They've elected me to their baseball hall of fame. There are not too many of them left.

I was in Brooklyn College when I was thirteen years old. I had skipped five times in public school, and I was in college when I was thirteen. They kicked me out in my junior year when I was fifteen. They said, "Make up your mind, baseball or books." All because I ran away with the Browns for a week or two at a time, they said, "You can't do that. You've got to stay in school." I said, "Well, I'll stick with baseball." So they kicked me out.

And today if you look in my office you'll see a beautiful plaque. They elected me to their hall of fame of Brooklyn College. In those days at Brooklyn College and City College, if you had high enough grades, and we didn't have any money of course, and I always had a ninety average or something like that.

Arthur Richman
159

That's how I got in.

At college the people next to me, some of them were almost married. And I had nothing in common with them. And my mama wouldn't let me go to Brooklyn all by myself. She'd make my father take me by train. I'm still close to Brooklyn College. I set up a foundation there in my brother's name. They list me as a graduate in anything they do, because I give quite a bit.

I have photos with the two Bushes and a photo with Nixon. I traveled in the military.

The Yankees came to St. Petersburg in 1973. The Mets were training there. I was in the hotel, and I saw this guy just standing there. He didn't seem to know anybody. So I went over and introduced myself, and he introduced himself [George Steinbrenner]. I said, "If there's anything, just tell me if you need anything." And one thing led to another.

Arthur Richman

Buck Showalter is manager of the Texas Rangers. He was the 2004 American League Manager of the Year. Previously he managed the New York Yankees and the Arizona Diamondbacks. Showalter had the 1994 Yankees in first place with a six and half game lead when the players' strike ended the season. When the 1995 Yankees made it to postseason competition, it was the first time for the franchise since 1981. Showalter was the youngest manager in the major leagues each year he was with the Yankees. His tenure as Yankee manager was the longest since Ralph Houk had the job in 1966-1973. With Arizona in 1999, Showalter led the team to a first-place finish with a 14-game lead, the first time in history that an expansion team had won a title in as few as two years.

Buck Showalter

In basketball, I can come every time and say: give the ball to Michael Jordan. In football I can say, always hand the ball to Gayle Sayres. In baseball I can't have Mike Young take the first at-bat every inning. I can't have my closer pitch every inning. It's seven or eight months.

Baseball teaches the importance of sacrifice. What other sport uses the word, "sacrifice"? We have the sacrifice bunt and the sacrifice fly. We count them. They're stats. And they're good. What other sport has anything like that?

In baseball, every year we play two hundred games, counting spring training. You play so many games. Every strength and weakness on every club will show up. Whatever weakness there is, it will show up. And whatever strength you have will show up.

Sometimes in my job I might have to sacrifice one game for the ability to win two, and get two out of three on the road. No other sport promotes the big picture like that, to not get too involved in one situation or one game. That is what's different about our game. The one thing we do, from a team standpoint, is get to

Buck Showalter

What other sport uses the word, "sacrifice"? We have the sacrifice bunt and the sacrifice fly. We count them. They're stats. And they're good. What other sport has anything like that?

Buck Showalter

the playoffs.

When the playoffs come around, then everything is different. The guys that have been the most successful in the regular season, especially the managers, may need to change something. The guys and methods who got you there may not be exactly right for that one short series. What we try to do with a one-game view is different. The most successful manager might be the one who will roll the dice.

John Smoltz is the all-time leader for wins and strikeouts in postseason championship competition. He is a seven-time All-Star. Smoltz and Hall-of-Famer Dennis Eckersley are the only two pitchers in history to accumulate both 150 wins and 150 saves, and Smoltz is the only one to return to All-Star status as a starting pitcher after making the conversion from starter to ace reliever. Smoltz missed the entire 2000 season after an elbow injury requiring reconstructive surgery.

John Smoltz

This line of work is not reality to a lot of people. The rules and reality are thrown out the window when you make more money than people think you should make, by doing something that everybody else thinks they would do for free.

People think, "Well, they're making this much." And people think, when you make that much money, that rules and reality don't apply to you, and that everything is fine, and you don't have any problems. If you make a certain level of money, everyone thinks everything is fine, and you don't have the same problems or other issues as other people, or go through the same things other people go through.

The biggest thing in our sport is perseverance. How many people think of perseverance in sports that make us a lot of money? I personally think of perseverance because I'm at a different level. When people see somebody come back from something, what do they think? It's like, "This guy just came back from a horrific injury; look at his perseverance. Maybe I can do that in my own job or in my own life." But if they don't get past the money and the high living then their reality is skewed. You have to separate that. Think how many times you hear, "This is the price you pay.

John Smoltz

If you make a certain level of money, everyone thinks everything is fine, and you don't have the same problems or other issues as other people, or go through the same things other people go through.

John Smoltz

This is the way you are. This is the price you pay for fame. This is what you're supposed to do."

I think of characteristics within the game that teach me lessons for life, not so much values but lessons. Having gone through so many of them, I don't think anything could happen outside baseball that I wouldn't be prepared to handle.

You should never let the situation dictate who you are or what you do. You can either choose to be a victim of circumstances or you can choose to attack the circumstances, all sorts of circumstances. That's what I've always tried to do. A lot of my perspectives are different from most.

In '91, I learned: never give up, don't give up. Never think of giving up. I was 2-11 in the first half. But you don't give up. I turned around and had a great second half, and pitched the seventh game of the World Series. So I learned a lot from that.

John Smoltz

Mike Stanton ranks number one for most games pitched among all active players, and he ranks seventh all-time for most games pitched. He has been to the World Series with the Atlanta Braves and the New York Yankees, and he has also pitched for the Boston Red Sox, Texas Rangers, and Washington Nationals. In six World Series he has a 3-0 record with a 1.54 ERA.

Mike Stanton

There's a reason why you watch your children play sports, and it's got very little to do with the actual sport. It doesn't matter what the sport is. It's something that teaches you discipline. It teaches you how to be a team player, how to put the team before yourself. Everyone has said that baseball is a team sport, but it's a team sport for what the individuals do. In order for the team to win, each individual does their job. The important part is still the team.

You could put up the best numbers in the world. It doesn't do any good if you don't win; then it's all for nothing. It's something kind of hard to explain, especially when you're trying to instill it in your children.

I've been blessed with being on some very good teams that have been to the postseason several times. The common denominator in all those teams is that even if you do have superstars on the team, those superstars all have one common goal in sight, and that's the team. Now, you have guys that put up the numbers and that help the team win, but there are some instances, some situations where you might have to sacrifice those numbers

Mike Stanton

I've been blessed with being on some very good teams that have been to the postseason several times. The common denominator in all those teams is that even if you do have superstars on the team, those superstars all have one common goal in sight, and that's the team.

Mike Stanton

for the team to win. The teams that win have guys who understand that and that are willing to do that.

It starts from the top, from the very top, like Mr. Steinbrenner. As a player there is really only one thing you can ask for from an owner, and that is that he's going to do everything to help your team win. And there's been a lot of talk about George, how he's got the money to do this, and he's got the money to do that. It's not all about money. Money doesn't make the team win. It helps.

You have to put quality people on the field, and have quality on and off the field, and that's something the Yankees have taken great pride in, to make sure the guys they put out there are going to do what they have to do to help the team. There are a lot of great ballplayers that I don't think that the Yankees would like to have, because they may not fit that mold of what the organization is looking for.

One of the other common denominators that those teams have had is that, if nothing else, we love to play the game. Everyone kind of makes a big deal about how much we make,

Mike Stanton

and I've said this several times. I hope people believe it. I know it's kind of hard to believe: I wouldn't do this for the money. There's a lot of down sides to baseball that people don't see. The amount of time we're away from our families, the horrific travel schedule, and the toll on your body playing every day, absolutely every day. Those are things that don't seem like much on paper, until you have to go through it yourself.

Mike Stanton

Alan Trammell had a 20-year playing career with the Detroit Tigers, joining Ty Cobb and Al Kaline as the only players with that distinction. Trammell was a six-time All-Star and was the 1984 World Series Most Valuable Player. When his playing career ended he had more home runs and a higher fielding percentage than any Hall-of-Fame shortstop. Trammell worked as the first base coach for the San Diego Padres and as the hitting coach for the Tigers. He managed the Tigers for three years, 2003-2005.

Timing is everything, and I'm sure you've heard from everyone about hard work.

If you fail, there's another day to come back. Knowing that comes from experience. I think a lot of players will say that they don't really understand that. Fortunately, I learned that even before getting to pro ball. I think once I got into pro ball, I was able to take it to another level. Once you get into professional baseball, that's your job and you're playing every day, not like in high school where you play a couple days a week and practice a few times a week or even college where you're practicing more. Basically, in professional baseball, even if you're in the minor leagues, you play almost every day, six days a week.

I went through trials and tribulations like everybody does, but was able to grasp that, knowing there's another day to come back, a little sooner than most, probably. I came up to the big leagues at nineteen. I was able to understand that a little bit, and I was able to stay. A lot of people come up at an early age, but they're not able to stay. Fortunately, I was able to stay.

Alan Trammell

*If you fail,
there's another day
to come back.*

*Nobody has a crystal ball.
But [in 1984] we knew that we
were going to be good.*

Alan Trammell

Not just in baseball, in all parts of life, you have to listen, absorb a lot, and try certain things. Sometimes what you hear or what you try might not be for you, but from experience you learn to weed out certain things. I don't know if there's any other way than from experience.

You're going to get a lot of advice as a young person. You're probably going to try a lot of different things, but not everything will be for you. Through experience you have to try different things, be smart enough to realize: yes, that is for me, or: no, that's not for me. And then put that stuff aside and continue on with the stuff you like. Trial and error, I believe it works for all of us.

In 1984 [with the Tigers] it was a special year for us. We learned about hard work. We had been working at it for a couple years. The year before in '83 we were knocking at the door, and Baltimore of course beat us out down the stretch. They ended up winning the World Series. But the next year, then we came to spring training thinking this was our year, and it happened to be. We got off to a good start, a very good start, 35 and 5. But

Alan Trammell
177

again, it was the hard work that Sparky [Anderson] had put in.

He had said when he came to Detroit that it would take five years, and it was the fifth year. It doesn't always work quite like that. It sounds good. It makes for a good story. He knew what he was doing. He knew that it was just a matter of time before we could reach that point. We had the right man to teach us. It was a realistic goal. I mean we knew we were going to be good, whether or not we were going to win a World Championship. Nobody has a crystal ball. But we knew that we were going to be good.

Alan Trammell

Jimy Williams is a special instructor for the Tampa Bay organization. He has 28 years experience as a coach or manager, including twelve years as a major-league manager with the Toronto Blue Jays, Boston Red Sox, and Houston Astros. In 1999 with the Red Sox, Williams was named American League Manager of the Year.

Sometimes a really good effort is what results in an error. I just want to see the effort.

Jimy Williams

Don't have expectations. Never expect anything specific. Every year and every game starts zero-zero. You never know what to expect. That's why you go and play.

Always think about career longevity. That's why we care about pitch counts. That's why we care about a pitcher's delivery: longevity. That's what to strive for in all pitchers, that they can pitch a long time.

Never compare players. It isn't fair to either player. Focus on effort. If a player gives his best effort, that's what matters. He might make an error. Sometimes a really good effort is what results in an error. I just want to see the effort.

Jimy Williams

Don Zimmer is the last remaining player for the Brooklyn Dodgers, who still wears a baseball uniform at work. Zimmer has been in professional baseball since 1949. He was a player with the Dodgers and four other major-league teams from 1954 through 1965, and then served as a minor-league coach. He has been a major-league coach or manager continuously since 1971. Zimmer became manager of the San Diego Padres in 1972. He also managed the Boston Red Sox, Texas Rangers, and Chicago Cubs and was elected National League Manager of the Year in 1989. Zimmer worked as the bench coach for the New York Yankees under Joe Torre for eight years. Zimmer became a senior advisor and coach for Tampa Bay in 2004.

Don Zimmer

You become prominent in baseball, naturally. Everybody in the world knows who you are. Even when you take a guy like Yogi Berra. He's been out of the game, how long? And every time you look up he's on some commercial. That prominence comes from being in baseball, plus being a great player. It opens up a lot of avenues to work for big companies.

It's amazing what people will do when they see an athlete. It's just something special. It opens up a lot of avenues for things to do down the line. I mean: there aren't many ballplayers that can move into an office and run a company, because all he's ever done is play baseball. But the name can be used.

You take Joe Torre. Here's a man that, several years ago, I didn't know if he would go into the Hall of Fame, playing-wise. But now, with the playing and the World Series success, this man is going to go into the Hall of Fame. Joe Torre's name is at the top of the game, and it should be.

Don Zimmer

Much depends on where you go. He's in the biggest place in the world right now, New York. He's been tremendous for the city, for the Yankees, for the media.

Joe has handled a lot of situations. In all the years, you're not going to see Joe make a bad statement. He's too smart for that. He knows how to choose words. He knows how to handle people. And when you win with that, it's just another plus. He knows how to handle men, and I think that sums it up.

Don Zimmer

ADVERSITY

Adversity engenders patience and perseverance. Patience and perseverance build up experience and character, and character is the source of the hopeful optimism that leads to our finest achievements. The initial responses to adversity - patience and perseverance - are complex and dynamic. Patience by itself may suggest passive acceptance or resignation. But there is another kind of patience that operates on a higher plane, beyond the present circumstances, an attitude that does not rise and fall with the ups and downs of present circumstances. Good patience rests on the knowledge (from history) that a means of enduring has been found by those who went before us. Overcoming adversity means transforming it. What was an obstacle becomes a stepping-stone. Perseverance begins with an aggressive examination of the adverse conditions and continues with acknowledgment of what may be painful, creative thinking about ways to address and overcome these conditions, and experimentation through trial and error to learn what works and what doesn't work in the present situation. Over time, adversity becomes a means to growth and development. As we face and overcome diverse difficulties, we become stronger and wiser as a result. Just being aware of this process creates the possibility of positive responses to almost any kind of adversity.

ANXIETY

Anxiety arises from the unknown. Adversity can push us suddenly into the realm of the unknown, which is why we often feel anxiety when encountering adversity. Facing adversity and engaging the most difficult circumstances will always bring knowledge. Knowledge reduces the unknown, and by reducing the unknown we can reduce our anxiety.

CAREER

Focus on longevity. Stay in shape. Keep your skills sharp, and keep developing new skills. Think beyond your present situation. There is always something coming later. What do want to be doing in five years? What will be necessary for you to get from where you are today, to where you want to be in five years? What is your plan to see that those necessities will be addressed?

COMPETITION

To compete means, etymologically, to seek together. Competition is good, and competition is a zero-sum proposition only in the narrowest sense for the shortest time frame. Good competitors will elevate your performance and make you better at what you do. The competitive environment is a form of constructed adversity. Competition brings out the best in us. Competition stimulates effort and leads to improvement.

COMMUNICATION

Effective communication is one way to take the initiative in any circumstances. Communication is an essential element in teamwork. Other people rely on you to be where you are supposed to be, at the right time, and do the right thing. Timely communication avoids surprises and disappointments. Within any team environment there is always communication going on, whether it is explicit or not. Thinking actively about what to communicate, and how, will increase the quality and quantity of communication. In addition to its own internal communications, every team also communicates to the outside world. Effective teams speak with one voice. Individual communications to the outside world should not interfere with the theme of univocal team communication.

DISCIPLINE

A person with discipline is, literally, one who has been taught. In baseball contexts, discipline refers to good habits of conduct and attitude. Discipline includes preparation, punctuality, practice with a set routine, and commitment to peak physical condition. Discipline includes acceptance of responsibility. Discipline is a source and cause of improvement. Repetition refines skills and also yields benchmarks for future reference and measuring improvements. Discipline becomes more important in the team context and most important as a leadership quality. If you cannot discipline and manage yourself, forget about managing others.

Themes

EFFORT

Effort is the way to maximize the probability of success and minimize the probability of regret. The biggest regrets often arise from an awareness that one could have done more and yet didn't, when there is no chance to go back and try again. Maximum effort rules out that type of regret. Maximum effort helps you learn what you can control and what you can't control. Maximum effort brings you to the point of knowing rather than guessing what you are capable of doing.

FAILURE

Nobody has a good day every day. In baseball failure is ubiquitous. If we find that we are succeeding more often than not, then our definition of success needs adjustment. We do better when we are challenged. Failure being the norm stimulates effort and creativity. Continuous learning comes from continuous examination of outcomes that are less than ideal. While dwelling on failure is counterproductive, learning a lesson before moving on is often essential. Failure never occurs in a vacuum. No one is ever alone in failure. Learn from mistakes. Ask the question, "What did I do wrong?" Get a complete answer. Consider what can be learned from it. And then move on.

FOCUS

Distractions impair performance. In any given situation, no matter how complex, at any given moment there will be relatively few factors requiring actual attention or action. Success depends on being able to filter out the hundreds or even thousands of extraneous factors that simply do not matter at that particular moment, and remove them from consciousness. This skill depends on both an innate capacity to focus and extensive practice developing the right ways of thinking.

FRIENDS

Choose your friends carefully. Choose people with good moral traits such as honesty, courage, reliability, and a temperate disposition. Be careful that you do not passively let others choose you to be their friends. People with problems and bad habits will often seek out others and attempt to bring others down to their level. Notice how people live their lives. Examine the quality of their relationships and how they interact with strangers as well as with their friends and acquaintances.

GRATITUDE
Much of what we enjoy is unearned and unmerited. Gifts and talents are unearned except to the extent that we exercise and develop them. Be grateful to people who help you, even if it seems as if they were only doing their job. Give credit to people who teach you something. Express gratitude. Don't keep it to yourself.

HISTORY
Knowledge of history increases your capacity to make wise decisions. Most of history is about decision-making: who made what decisions, why, and what outcomes resulted. Every person has a history. Knowing something about a person's history will help you interact with them, no matter what the circumstances.

HONESTY
Any form of pretense, at best, will consume energy. Maintaining a façade can easily consume energy to the point of making a person weak and ineffective. Truth and simplicity help a person to be strong and effective. Honesty is one of the observable virtues that can help us choose our friends and companions. People who lack honesty will be unable to function as friends in some of the most important areas, such as offering constructive criticism.

HUMILITY
Humility and true success often come together. People who brag about their achievements usually are not successful and know that they are not successful, which is why they talk so much. Since no one succeeds all the time, failure humbles everyone eventually. Humility makes room for patience and flexibility, which make room for success.

LEARNING

Learning never ends. The wise approach to learning and education is continuous improvement. Improvement is manifest in making continuous adjustments, little changes that get better results. Continuous incremental adjustment is one way to deal with circumstances that may seem unchangeable.

LIMITS

If we don't go too far at least once, we don't know where our limits are. It is possible to be too cautious, too timid. Once we know how far we can go, then we can live within our known limits. If we don't know our limits, then we must live with some artificial, assumed limits.

LUCK

Luck is real, meaning that results are not always attributable to reasons that can be identified. While we may understand the causative factors in any given situation, there will always be an element of mystery. Accept good luck with humility and gratitude. Engage bad luck with an exaggerated willingness to accept responsibility for outcomes that were actually beyond your control. By opening your thinking to consider what might have been your fault, even when it seems highly unlikely to have been so, you might learn something. It is bad luck to think much about other people's failures and shortcomings.

MONEY

There is no quantity of money that equates to success in life. There is no quantity of money that can produce happiness. Accumulating a lot of money can lead to complacency and failure. Many talented people have failed to get the best results from their talent because they achieved a certain level of wealth too quickly and too easily.

PARENTS

Parents have an almost unlimited potential to shape their children for better or worse. Parents are the first teachers and set the tone for the child's future experience of all teachers. Wisdom gets passed from generation to generation through the investment of time and effort.

PATIENCE
Patience relaxes you and allows you to think more clearly and make better decisions. Patience develops more easily within an understanding that failure is the norm. When we understand success as something that doesn't happen frequently, patience can include active waiting and watching for opportunities. (See also Adversity.)

PERSPECTIVE
The only actions that matter are those we take from this moment forward. Every hour brings us a fresh start if we are willing to embrace it. Focus on what is in front of you right now, knowing there is always another day and another situation. Wisdom is deeply connected to having and maintaining a sense of perspective.

PRIDE
There is a huge difference between having a strong sense of self and indulging in pride. A strong sense of self engenders patience, flexibility, friendliness, and ability to focus appropriately in every situation. Pride makes a person impatient, inflexible, and too often focused on the self instead of what is happening at that moment.

PUNCTUALITY
Punctuality shows your teammates what you think of them. The question is about attitude rather than perfunctory appearance.

SELFISHNESS AND UNSELFISHNESS
Attaining the capacity to help other people, and then exercising this capacity wisely, is the highest form of success. When you give to others, good things happen. Selfishness prevents good things from happening. Selfishness works against the team's success and therefore against all true success. Ultimately

Themes

selfishness is always self-defeating. Unselfishness derives joy from the success of others. Since there are so many other people and just one self, unselfishness immediately offers a multitude of opportunities for happiness.

STRENGTHS AND WEAKNESSES
Know your own strengths. Accept them. Develop them. Be grateful for them. Face up to your weaknesses emphatically. Regard weaknesses as the biggest opportunities for significant improvement. Focus more on your weaknesses and work harder addressing your weaknesses than you do developing your strengths. Practice and discipline can mitigate all weaknesses and eliminate many of them.

SUCCESS
Be careful about defining success. There are a lot of bad definitions in circulation, and more coming along all the time: you should have this, or you should do that. The most seductive definitions are those that promise a good outcome once and for all: if you can just achieve X, then everything will be fine forever. Real success is more of an attitude and condition than an event that can be observed. How do you know if you have had a good day? Keep asking yourself this question, and don't let yourself off with an easy answer. If you find yourself defining most days as being successful, your standards might be too low. There is always a higher level. As you succeed at one level and move up to the next, success becomes more difficult.

TALENT
Talent is like a set of tools in a box. You have to open the box, take out the tools, and learn how to use them. Take lessons from someone who knows more than you do, and pick someone who is a good teacher as well as an expert. Then practice, practice, and practice. A worker with inferior tools but with more knowledge of how to use them will usually get better results than one who has better tools but hasn't developed the skills to use them well.

TEACHING AND TEACHERS

Usually the best teachers are people who did not have the most talent. People who have had to work hard and think hard, to make the most of difficult circumstances, know a lot about overcoming adversity. The best teachers can empathize with those who don't have the greatest talent. Teaching and learning occur in every human interaction, even when the persons involved are not cognizant of this reality. Choosing the right teachers, formally and informally, is a skill in itself. How do you know whose advice to follow? Trial and error is one good method to find good teachers. Most people are more open-minded to receive teaching when things are going badly for them. When everything is fine and wonderful, the eagerness to learn and improve can diminish. Good teaching gives understanding. Good teaching requires much patience. Good teaching requires caring about those who can learn from you.

TEAMWORK

The most essential quality is subordination of self-interest to the good of the team, both in thinking and in doing. The team has a separate consciousness, distinct from all the individuals and bigger than the sum of all the individuals' consciousness. There are "team thoughts." The team consciousness can be developed through exercise and practice. The team develops its own voice (see Communication). Have a common goal. Articulate it. Communicate it. Think about it.

WINNING AND LOSING

Usually you learn more from losing than you do from winning. Losing is often a good outcome for the long term. Most people don't grow wise as result of everything being fine and wonderful all the time. Losing usually produces better learning. When you lose, you learn about yourself. Winning is a journey that never ends. There is always another level. Winning is a state of mind. Aiming too low in the beginning is one way to guarantee losing. The best competitors are focused on the highest conceivable outcome from the first moment.

Themes